VOLUME ONE

# PINCHES
# OF WISDOM

**Also by Glynn Cardy ...**

*A Book of Blessings*
(Melbourne: Coventry Press, 2020)

*Love and Other Blessings*
(Melbourne: Coventry Press, 2023)

It's a gem! When reading *Pinches of Wisdom*, my senses become less dull, more alive, and quietly humoured. My heart becomes fuller, deeper, and more able to bear the suffering of the world. Magically and with the lightest of touch, the book acts as a conduit in reconnecting readers to their own wisdom and to act within the integrity of love and clarity, justice, and peace.

Amaradipa/Minh Truong-George
Ordained Buddhist/Psychotherapist

Wisdom comes in many ways, along many paths, from the ordinary and the unexpected, the ancient and the contemporary. In these Pinches, Glynn encapsulates that and, whatever our spiritual background, encourages us to see and hear wisdom in everyday life; a gift we can all embrace for our own wellbeing and the world's.

Caro Penney
Warden at Iona Abbey
on behalf of the Iona Community

Over and over in the Christian scriptures we are told to 'pay attention!', 'wake up!', 'look!', 'listen!'.
It is only when we do this that we'll begin to understand our place in the world and might begin to notice the work of the Divine in our lives and in the lives of those around us.
With careful attention to those things that often happen just on the periphery of our vision, Glynn Cardy has given us a collection of stories that point us to how we might live – fully, authentically and honestly.
For those of us who are part of the church in this season, Glynn shows us how we might engage in the world: perhaps we might watch and listen and learn more and be slower to pronounce and pontificate. Regardless, it's not a bad way to live, whoever we are.
In her poem, 'Instructions for Living a Life', the poet Mary Oliver suggests that we should, 'Pay attention. Be astonished. Tell about it.' Glynn Cardy has taken this to heart and given us a gift that might point us to a life worth living.

Jeremy Greaves
Anglican Archbishop of Brisbane

VOLUME ONE

# PINCHES OF WISDOM

GLYNN CARDY

Published in Australia by
Coventry Press
33 Scoresby Road
Bayswater VIC 3153

ISBN 9781922589583

Copyright © Glynn Cardy 2024

All rights reserved. Other than for the purposes and subject to the conditions prescribed under the *Copyright Act*, no part of this publication may be reproduced, stored in a retrieval system, or transmitted in any form or by any means, electronic, mechanical, photocopying, recording or otherwise, without the prior permission of the publisher.

Catalogue-in-Publication entry is available from the National Library of Australia
http://catalogue.nla.gov.au

Cover design by Ian James – www.jgd.com.au
Cover photograph by Kirsty Antunovich
*Dog&Co. Photography*. Used by permission.
Text design by Coventry Press
Set in EB Garamond

Printed in Australia

# Contents

| | |
|---|---|
| Foreword | ix |
| Waiting | 1 |
| Pears | 3 |
| Birthdays | 5 |
| Bears | 8 |
| Wobbling | 10 |
| Butch | 12 |
| A Proposition | 14 |
| Friendship | 17 |
| Crosswalk | 19 |
| Helping | 22 |
| Pink Tulle | 24 |
| Glimpses | 26 |
| A Puppy | 28 |
| Mercy | 30 |
| Trucks | 32 |
| Readjustment | 34 |
| Flowers | 36 |
| At One | 39 |
| Christmas | 41 |
| Russ | 44 |
| Weddings | 47 |
| Playing | 50 |
| Stocktake | 53 |
| NZ's Finest | 56 |

| | |
|---|---|
| Blessed | 59 |
| Quiet | 61 |
| Ahh, Music | 63 |
| Backyards | 66 |
| Solidarity | 68 |
| Rainbows | 70 |
| The Tide | 72 |
| A Pyx | 74 |
| Disruptive Space | 76 |
| A Kransekake | 78 |
| A Laugh | 80 |

# Foreword

*Pinches of Wisdom* is a collection of everyday stories and thoughts about living. In these you will find many stories of friendship, tolerance, love and hope. Humour is rife. A few stories are about politics, a few about community, a few about religion, a few about music, and a few about walking around my local neighbourhood with Finn, the faithful hound. The question of spirituality – how we try to live a connected, purposeful and contented life – is present throughout.

This is not a religious book. God and church barely get a mention. And the dogma and deliberations that arise from God and church, even less so. Yet is a book that gives glimpses into how to live a life noticing and giving thanks for the little and quirky things, including the people we meet and who become part of our lives. It is a book full of glimpses of encouraging people, generosity, compassion and the power of humour.

I've been privileged to be a Christian parish minister for nearly 40 years. I've lived mainly in Aotearoa New Zealand, and mainly in urban environments. But the communities I've been a part of have been diverse. I spent 9 years in Glen Innes, at that time one of the economically poorer suburbs in New Zealand. I spent 11 years in Epsom, a leafy dormitory suburb known for the quality of its schools. I spent 9 years in downtown Auckland at a church that was a home for pretty much anyone who didn't fit elsewhere. And for the last decade, I've been part of the Community of St Luke in Remuera, a community whose commitment to justice and care is frequently at odds with its affluent neighbourhood.

I've also spent shorter periods of time working in rural parishes, including in England. Each place has extended to me a warmth and welcome, sharing its insights, and shaping me into who I am. In each place, I've had to learn its unique language of listening and relating. I've had to discover the environment – physical, social and political – and how that impacts on people for the better or worse. I've had to learn the silences of each place, the hospitality and joy of each place, and the pinches of wisdom found in each place.

Being a minister isn't about God and church. It's about people. It's always been about people. And God and church are, at their best, code words for love and community. Love and community being, of course, always about people.

I would like to thank all those who have contributed to this book through their encouragement, humour and insights. I'd like to thank Hugh McGinlay and the team at Coventry Press. I'd like to thank the parish of St Luke in Remuera. I'd like to thank my family, and our dog Finn who gets me out walking the streets. Most of all I'd like to thank my wife and soulmate, Stephanie, for the many and constant pinches of wisdom she has flavoured our life with over the last 40 years.

# Waiting

I WAS AT THIS GAS STATION, doubling as a drink station. In the hinterland of Spain. Nowhere and nothing much country. Just road, hills, and gold-brown earth. And it was hot. Seriously hot. 39 degrees of seriousness.

So, after drinking my expresso, I head to the bathroom, as you do. It's locked. There's this big Spanish guy at a nearby table, also gleaming with perspiration, who shrugs at me. He's in the queue, the queue of two, he and me.

And we wait. And wait. Women come and go from the other cubicle, but we wait. And wait.

It's tempting, of course, to head round the back, as guys have done from time immemorial. But we look at one another and silently decide to tough it out.

Something serious must be happening in that male cubicle. Probably some poor guy with a problem. Enough said. So, we wait.

Finally, the door opens. And a woman walks out.

The Spanish guy simultaneously raises his hands and shrugs as if to say 'Well, what do you know...,' and I respond in kind.

The woman laughs. And we laugh.

It was one of those moments. A moment that transcends culture and language.

When you think about it, we spend a lot of our life waiting. Waiting for the bathroom. Waiting in queues. Waiting in traffic. Waiting in a medical reception room. Waiting for a child, partner, or parent. Waiting because the timing of each us is slightly different, as are our needs, as are our wants.

I often think the ritual of a wedding is important for what it teaches about waiting. And I'm not just referring to the notion that the bride arrives 'fashionably late' at the church. Weddings usually involve lots of expectations, lots of differences of opinion, lots of compromise, and, not infrequently, tears. They are a lesson in blending two family systems. And patience – waiting – is a big part of making a relationship work.

The trick to waiting is to momentarily put aside the reason you're waiting, and be cognisant of your surroundings. Like, in traffic, appreciating the time with others in your car, or listening to the radio. Like, in a medical waiting room, having time to quietly sit and think. Like, in a people queue, watching and smiling at the other people waiting like you're waiting. Like the big Spanish guy in the heat.

Consider for a moment the slow decline and death of letter writing. Remember the days of taking time to bring out pen and paper, to pause and compose before you wrote, and then to seal it and walk down the road to post? Remember the feel of the paper, one's ink-stained fingers, and the joy of receiving a handwritten letter?

While email and texts are very convenient for lots of mundane and business communications, the patience and pondering needed for a letter to a dear friend far away is not well served, or often well kept, by our modern devices.

Again, it seems to come down to waiting, doing things more slowly, going more slowly, and the patience needed for it. While I'm not a Luddite, I do wonder whether we have lost the skills for, and the blessing of, waiting.

# Pears

THERE ARE THREE PEAR TREES along the road from my house. Their branches reach out and dangle their leaves and fruit close to the footpath.

Pear trees like sunny spots. And they don't like wind. They also need looking after – feeding with mulch and being watered by committed gardeners. To get the sweet treat of a juicy pear you need to do the mahi (work).

Or you can pinch one. A pear treat that is.

And that was a problem for the three pear trees along the road with their dangling branches and their committed green guardians.

Now, a little about the guardians. They are little. Pre-schoolers. Supported by teachers and parents with gardening genes and dirt in their fingernails. Yes, the trees are on the edge of a kindergarten. And the kids love their pear trees.

Fun fact: pear trees in Aotearoa NZ can grow up to 12 metres high. Lots of potential for climbing, and shade, and all those good feelings that trees can give if only we let them. Which many kids do.

Next fun fact: a pear tree in Aotearoa NZ can produce in one season up to 40 kgs of fruit. Which is about 241 pears per tree. So potentially this dendritic threesome could produce 723 pears per year! Which is more than one pear per child in the kindergarten, and more than one pear per every family member of every child in the kindergarten, and more than one pear per teacher and their families too, and more than all the above combined! It's a lot of pears.

A not fun fact: there are lots of hungry people in our city. Although most of us, most of the time, kind of pretend that this isn't so, or is only so for a few, or isn't so in our neighbourhood, though the evidence from foodbanks and charities says otherwise. People are hungry, some in every suburb and lots in others.

Children are hungry too. They need pears, and more besides. So, somebody with a heart and a brain and a vision at that kindergarten did something extraordinary. They put up a sign. Which didn't say 'Keep your hands off our fruit!' Or 'Grow your own!' Or 'Thieves will be prosecuted!' Instead, their sign invited passers-by, if they were hungry, to take one, and then do something in exchange. And that was to leave a note, card and pen provided, to thank the little green guardians for their mahi.

The deal was: have a treat and do the mahi of saying thanks. The pear was a gift, and so was the card of thanks. Gift for gift. Such exchanges allow for dignity.

So, I wrote a note.

Only the pears weren't in season, and I wasn't hungry. My treat was seeing their sign and thinking of the generosity of spirit it reflected. So, I wrote them a little note saying I thought they were all wonderful and I hoped that they would plant lots and lots of fruit trees in their lives, here, there and everywhere, and teach others how to plant and care for trees, and share the fruit with as many people as possible, and get lots and lots of cards, and make people who walk by like me feel good.

I had to write on the back of the card as well as the front to get all that in.

Last fun fact: Samuel Marsden, the first European missionary to Aotearoa, planted the first and oldest pear tree in 1819. It's a beauty. Up at Kerikeri in the Bay of Islands.

And Marsden had a mixed press back then, which is reflected in the mix of opinions about him even to this day. But he did have the good sense to plant a tree. Which has fed and brought joy to lots and lots of people over a lot of years.

# Birthdays

MY BIRTHDAY IS ABOUT TO ARRIVE. Again. Not a particularly momentous one. Just one of those regular post-60 ones. The sort that sneaks up on you and suddenly there's a numerical change.

Not that I feel any different, of course. Or remember what I felt like a year ago. Or the year before that. Like most of us, I don't mark time or, usually, memories that way.

Rather time and memories are marked by things like children growing through their stages of life, or places we've lived or worked, or holidays, or animals. Indeed, last year could have been called 'Year of the Dog'.

For Finn, our Red Golden Retriever, every day is a birthday. A day to eat, drink, wag, lick, and be merry. And the more people who come to visit the happier he is, and the more unruly he is until everyone has been bounced into belonging. It's all about belonging. And having fun while doing it.

Birthdays in the best sense are markers not so much of aging but of belonging. When family or friends gather to share some food, some cake, and maybe wee gifts, they are in a sense saying that we belong together. They're saying not just that we are related or that we like you, but that you matter to us. And not because of anything you've done particularly. You matter because our lives are interconnected and if you weren't here, we would be the poorer.

Of course, when you were a child, you probably didn't frame your understanding of birthdays this way. Presents, food, and games, I guess, featured more prominently. My childhood birthdays were invariably shared with a brother. (Yes, this is birthday week in the Cardy whānau* with three siblings, one son, and one niece all born within the space of four days!)

As you grew into a teenager, I suspect friends began to feature more prominently. Good friends, special friends, and would-be friends. And you came to believe that birthdays were about pleasing friends as much as pleasing yourself. Which is sort of true, and sort of not.

Then there were birthdays that coincided with life events. Completing high school, a university degree or two, a first job. Flatting, getting serious with someone, moving in together, maybe marriage. Maybe children.

For those of us who have the privilege and responsibility of children, the notion of birthday changes forever. For a starter, you remember their birth day. The wonder and joy of it. And the relief of a safe arrival.

Then as the years tick by, there is the hosting of parties. Little chairs and tables. Costumes. Face paint. Fairy bread. Chocolate crackles. Cakes featuring pirates or princesses or whatever Disney movie is in vogue. Lots of running, squeals of delight, grandparents taking photos, and dad supervising the cooking of home-made spaghetti pizzas and sausage rolls. And then the dog vacuuming up whatever morsel he could find.

Hosting birthdays as children grow and change supersedes your own birthday. And this is a good thing. For most of us reach a stage when turning a year older loses its earlier appeal. That stage when we'd like to shed possessions or pounds rather than acquire more. Where dressing up, drinking up, and eating rich food, lose their former allure. Though a chuckle, or an embrace, or a moment of being known in the heart of another... well, these never lose their appeal.

Mind you, the mid-lifers, in the so-called crisis years of trying things differently, might want to acquire, splurge, and indulge in some excess. But – according to the psychology books – I'm beyond that now, well and truly having skidded into my sixties with all the pot-holes and surprises that decade brings.

Which brings me back to belonging. Birthdays were always about belonging. It's just that in getting older we kind of see it more clearly now. We celebrate the person who was born years before because we are connected to them. And such connections matter. More than anything else.

Through all the thin and thick of life, dodging those pot-holes, splashing through them, or falling smack bang on our faces, we are glad we're not alone. We are glad we are connected. Mud, muck, and all. And we are glad that our real wealth in life is not in what we possess but who we have had for company.

*whānau is a Māori word meaning family, extended family.*

# Bears

THE IDEA WAS BORN around a kitchen table, deep in the Cotswolds, 2006. I can't remember whose idea it was. I can't remember any dissent either. We just agreed that the bears should be invited to church.

We lived in a village of maybe 40 houses. Cotswoldian stone, wild flowers, and a pub. We weren't on a tourist route. The church was a Victorian remnant, with about 20 people, 40 on a good day, and usually no bears.

Even in deepest rural England, there is a bush telegraph. Someone, somehow, down in London, in the high and illustrious offices of *The Times* heard about our invitation. Then other papers got in on the act. Not that the bears made front page – more like page 5 where the quirky stories appeared.

We called it "The Blessing of the Teddy Bears". Which was nicely ambiguous about who was doing the blessing. Were we blessing the bears, or the bears us, or the divine both?

A reporter rang asking, "How can you bless something that isn't real?" Good question. What is real? What is a blessing?

Those of us from around the kitchen table weren't sure how our fellow villagers would respond. I mean the bears hadn't been invited before. Would our neighbours think it all childish? Or even irreverent? Would the bears even want to come to church?

On the morning of the blessing service, I spied Major Parker coming up the walk. He was an elderly aristocratic gentleman who lived in the big house. Well, actually, he only lived in a small part of it. Big houses aren't particularly friendly to the elderly.

Major Parker was known for two things. First, he was invariably kind and softly spoken. Secondly, he'd spent a good part of his war in Colditz, the site of Oflag IV-C, a prisoner-of-war camp for incorrigible Allied officers who had repeatedly escaped from other camps.

Needless to say, he was well liked in the village.

That morning of the bears, I noticed Major Parker coming up the path, through the cemetery, to the church door. With one hand he supported himself with his walking stick, and with the other hand he tenderly carried a small bear. And I knew then, that whatever else followed, a blessing was about to arrive.

To answer *The Times* reporter, I think 'real' is what has or does sustain us. And a blessing is both giving thanks for that 'real', and encouraging more of it.

Years later, during the Covid-19 pandemic in New Zealand when the whole country was told to stay home, stay safe, and walk around the block for our sanity, bears appeared. First there was just one or two. Then more, and more. They popped up in people's windows, waving to those walking by, and encouraging them.

There is a magic about Teddy Bears that is not just restricted to children.

# Wobbling

I WAS OUT ON MY AFTERNOON WALK around the neighbourhood when I saw him. He was hard to miss. On his veranda, going for it. In a bright orange, close-fitting T-shirt. With some music, I guess, coming through the earmuffs attached to his head. Doing his thing. Gyrating. Wobbling.

And he had a robust middle to wobble. Which was hard to miss in that close-fitting T-shirt and all. Round and round, side to side, shaking it. Oblivious of any passerby, like me.

He also had the aid of a hula-hoop.

Do you remember those things?

Well, they're been around a while. At least from 500 BCE. Usually made of cane. Used for dance, ritual, story-telling, and for just generally having fun. There are reports of their use in many cultures, in many parts of the world. Fun is trans-cultural.

In the 1800s, the name Hula was appropriated from, yes you guessed right, Hawaii. In Norway, they set off the wriggle-rock craze. Wriggling and rocking? The brightly coloured plastic version came from California in the 1950s. Which sparked a craze, that went on and on and on, 'til it faded in the 1990s.

It washed up in my Auckland childhood in the '60s. Every kid wanted one. Bright plastic hoops blossomed on our street. It was the accessory to have.

Dad, being the practical sort of guy he was, and of course not wanting to spend money unnecessarily, said he'd make one. Which in a flash he did. Only trouble was I then became the only kid on the street with a hula hoop made of black PVC piping.

I quickly lost my interest in hula hooping.

Besides, I wasn't that good at it. And saw no compelling reason to get good at it. Some things I figured were best left to others. Kind of how I think about learning Cyrillic languages, calculus equations, and rhythmic gymnastics.

The others who do master wobbling, and these days go to those Les-Mills-type classes at their city gyms, extol the great benefits of it. Like burning calories, cardiovascular fitness, core strength, and balance.

They don't bother to mention fun. Which, if I remember right, was the chief motivation for hula hooping on our street.

What I admired about the bright orange wobbler on the veranda that afternoon is that he seemed totally unconcerned about spectators, the walkers by, like me. He didn't care about how he looked. He didn't care if others didn't like his dress sense or actions, or thought he was rather ridiculous.

He didn't care because he was having fun, and the fun was so good he wanted to just keep it going, no matter what the distractions, no matter what others thought. Fun was intoxicating.

I looked at others who were walking by and watching while pretending not to. They all had a smile on their faces.

Fun does that. It affects those around. Brightens our day. Puts a skip in our step.

Not that the guy in the bright orange T-shirt knew that. He was deep in the world of wobbling fun. Blessed be the unselfconscious wobblers!

# Butch

I WAS ADOPTED BY A DOG when I was 23. He was a neighbourhood dog in what was regarded by one journalist as the 'worst' state housing area in Auckland. Not that the dog, or I, considered our neighbourhood like that. With no fences, lots of children, lots of playtime, and lots of places to roam, it was in many ways a good place.

The dog had been christened 'Butch' by the local kids. They wanted him to be tough, because tough was how you survived. In local parlance, you were staunch.

The problem was Butch wasn't tough or staunch. Not in the I-love-to-fight way. He liked to socialise, make friends and playmates, and eat. Especially eat. He had Labrador genes. He also figured out that if he adopted me then his life goals would probably be met.

As for me, I had no experience with dogs. Cats yes, dogs no. And given that I walked most places back then, he just trailed along. So, he went to lectures, visited my parents, enjoyed the beach, went on protest marches, and came to church.

In his later years he came to church a lot. When I left that state housing neighbourhood Butch came too. Over the years, he endeared himself to parishioners in St Heliers, Glen Innes, and finally Epsom. The best bits about church were the children who patted and climbed all over him, and, of course, the biscuits after the service.

In Epsom, we lived next door to the church, an easy amble for a sociable dog. It was a picturesque church that hosted many weddings and funerals. Butch came to most. He would plant himself at the front in a statuesque manner. Brides would put his name on the order of service. He was on a TV show. Undertakers were fond of him. He was a character who loved people.

Many people find that there is something about an animal that makes a house a home. And many people who came to that church for funerals found that the simple presence of a dog sitting peacefully beneath a casket was comforting. Butch had a way of respecting the dead and those who mourned.

When he died, we decided to have a funeral. In the church. Some 100 people came. One of the undertakers generously offered, free of charge, to provide a casket (white, child size) and organise a couple of burly guys from one of the local cemeteries to come and dig a hole for him in our backyard. My two lasting memories of the day are the children at the front of the church speaking about him, and later everyone helping fill in the two-metre hole.

The reason I'm thinking about Butch – some 20+ years after his death – is that two days ago, at a funeral, I met one of the staff, now retired, from that generous undertaking company. She told me something that brought tears to my eyes. She simply said, "I remember your dog. We washed him and blow-dried him, before we put him in the casket".

In other words, they treated his body like they would treat a human body, washing and beautifying before laying out. And they did it knowing that the casket would not be opened and we would not see they had done this. And they never told. And he would not have been easy to wash. He weighed some 50 kg, and had an abundance of long hair.

This act of unseen and untold kindness and respect deeply moved and still moves me as I write. To care for one in a manner to give dignity and respect. To care for one who is not of your kin, clients, or species. To care for one who cannot repay you, and whose family do not know of your care.

This is an act of grace. A gift. An act of kindness without wanting any reciprocity. Human-kind at its best giving to one of the best of animal-kind.

# A Proposition

I RECEIVED A THANK-YOU CARD THE OTHER DAY from an older couple I know. They send me a card every year at about this time. On their wedding anniversary. For, as you might suspect, I took their wedding back in the day. And every year as part of their profound and abiding thankfulness of having found each other, they send me a card. And as well as giving me a nice appreciated feeling, it makes me think back to their wedding.

It was the second time of being married for both. They had grown children. Grandchildren too. Spread around overseas. Lots of them. The kids had got over any initial doubts that this was a good thing for dad or mum, grandpa or grandma. (Offspring have all sorts of feelings at times like this.) And they'd decided to come. All of them. And all their relations too. And then, being older, the couple had a lot of friends. So, they came too.

The couple didn't want too much fuss. They organised it themselves. They wanted it simple. No wedding party, tuxedos and gowns. But then again, everyone wanted to come. Like, this was going to be big. And so it was. The image I remember most clearly is this couple, surrounded by lots of love and goodwill, dancing with and smiling at each other as the night rolled on and on and on.

It's quite a different deal signing up for marriage with someone when you're past three score years. You're not going to have children; you've got any children you're going to have. You're not, probably, going to start some new career. You don't, hopefully, care too much about what others think about you. You don't have to impress people like you might've in the past. You kind of know what you want to make you happy, and who you want in your life. A marriage proposal at this time of life is different.

## A Proposition

Mind you, I'm not sure marriage proposals when the couple are younger are quite what the movies portray. You know, the guy going down on bended knee, saying 'Will you marry me?' and producing a ring with a rock attached. But does it really happen like that? Maybe she rather than he proposed. Maybe there was a bit of nudging along. Maybe she or he had interrupted and said 'Wait, don't ask me yet'. Yes or No are not the only options. Maybe she wanted to choose her own ring with rock?

And then, there was probably lots of angst. Lots of unspoken scary, doubting, or exciting moments. Probably accompanied by earnest conversations, tears and kisses. Lots of wondering whether this is really going to be the right thing to do, now and for the future. A wondering that doesn't really have an answer. And whether you're younger or older, two shes or two hes, logical reasoning about marriage can only take you so far. There comes a time when you have to follow your heart and leap. And where you land you land.

When you're older, and you've lived those three score years and ten, and have known a lot of joy and sorrow, feasting and heartburn in your life you might want to ask, 'Will you marry me?' a little differently.

Maybe you'd want to say something like this:

Will you come with me to the edge of the world, to dangle our feet off, lick yummy ice-creams, and listen to the night sky? It whispers, you know.

Will you come with me into that place of both great joy and great commitment of caring for others, often members of our families? A place where we will need one another, to steady one another, to encourage each other.

Will you come with me to that time when our health begins to falter? When what we've done can no longer be done. When what has always worked before, doesn't now. When we feel vulnerable.

## A Proposition

Will you come with me into the vast unfathomable mystery? To journey to places of faith, of heart, of wonder. To leave behind all the dogmas and their doings that are incompatible with love.

Will you come with me as we change? Maybe we'll grow fat or bent over, or lose our money or marbles. Maybe we'll grow conceited, or lazy, or grumpy. We might need help to respect and love our own selves.

Will you come with me to a place of trust where we hold tenderly each other's tears and fears, dreams and failures, and find in our mutuality a power and wisdom we've not known before?

Will you come with me? And may I come with you?

# Friendship

I SPENT THREE DAYS LAST MONTH with a group of men who, like me, are sixty something. We walked, talked, sat, ate, talked more, shared, argued, laughed, and ate some more. We do this every year. If we can.

We have some history together. We were at a theological college together nearly 40 years ago. Not that most have been in religious employ for decades. The rivers of our lives are braided, swerving around all sorts of shingle banks, weaving and parting, swift and slow, going somewhere we know not.

We notice the changes as the years go by. The music in cafés is louder. We like to read the news holding a paper. We don't like restaurants where there is any pressure to leave. There are things we can't eat though we'd like to, things we can eat but there are consequences, and things we eat that evoke a deep gratitude for being alive. Good food is divine.

We like to sit. We wear hats and sunglasses, for our eyes and skin are not what they once were. We have sensible footwear. We walk a lot. We forget things and laugh at our forgetfulness. We like to look at trees, clever and beautiful architecture, and anything odd and different.

We don't mind silence in our conversations. We can go from political to personal, to teasing to tears, all in the space of a few minutes. Laughter is what keeps this river of friendship flowing.

Once again, like every year, we traverse the edges of politics and religion, the travesty of ugly buildings, the tenacity needed to save our planet, and the tiny joys and humour found in each of our personal circumstances of love and the miracle of being loved.

The predictable argument over incentivising the economy was held, debated with passion and humour, with no consensus reached. That predictable argument is more than a couple of decades old, though the contours of it have changed. The posturing and policies of the newest crop of politicians were discussed, with much laughter, some seriousness, and a tad of respect for those who offer themselves for these roles.

Our perspective is that of Pākehā\* men who have lived more than six decades tumbling and turning, leaping and being pushed, into the maelstrom of a changing and beautiful Aotearoa New Zealand. There has been much loss, much change, much pain, and much joy. We have had a lot of experience with getting it wrong, and occasionally getting it right, with dying and crying, with happiness and making it. We now know how little we know. And how little others, who tell us they know, don't.

If we have any wisdom to add, it is simply the importance of loyalty, endurance and friendship. With a liberal sprinkling of laughter. Laughing together might not solve all the world's problems, but it sets the tone and keeps the melancholy at bay.

One of our number makes a Christmas cake each year. Preferably, two months before. The fruit is soaked for three days in brandy. (I think the three days is a religious hangover.) Even the nuts get the brandy treatment. Molasses is added, as well as the usuals. I think the cake has over 30 individual ingredients. Baking time is four and a half hours. Then it gestates. Weekly he injects in more brandy. Finally, there is the icing – butter, icing sugar, almond, and yes, more brandy.

Before Christmas Day, he cuts small slices of this cake, puts them in special little cartons, and mails them around the country.

I was thinking that this masterpiece of a cake could be a metaphor for friendship. The great variety, the messy and sticky bits of our lives, brought and stirred together, slow cooked, left to sit, infused with spirit at many points in the process, then shared and enjoyed.

---

\**Pākehā is a Maori word meaning New Zealander European.*

# Crosswalk

ON A COLD WINTER'S MORNING, well before dawn, we crept out of our homes on the housing estate in Glen Innes and headed down to our local hall. It was 1983.

The hall was on the other side of busy Crossfield Road, and the other side from our homes and the large playing fields. There was no crossing. There were no speed bumps. The cars would hoon down the road and the kids would dodge them. It was an accident waiting to happen.

Silly, really. Who would put a community hall on the other side of the road from where everyone lived?

It was more than silly. It was dispiriting. For over the months and years, we had written to Council, told Council's officers, and anybody else who would listen, that we needed a zebra crossing before someone got killed. Nothing happened. Nothing was promised. Nobody seemed to care. We waited and waited and waited.

So that cold winter morning about 20 kids and parents did something. I can't remember whose idea it was. But it caught on quick. Someone got a measuring tape and chalk, someone got brushes, someone else got paint. Then feeling a little bit naughty and a big bit determined, we went out in the dark and painted a zebra crossing on Crossfield Road.

And it felt good. Really good. It warmed our hearts and our spirits. A community in action.

Then two days later, Council trucks with big burly fellas and water-blasters arrived. And that was the end of our zebra crossing.

But you know what, within a year there was a new hall built, on our side of the street.

Sometimes community action from the neighbourhood, by the neighbourhood, for the neighbourhood, with a little paint, lifts the spirits of the community, and occasionally gets a great result.

As I recall that story, I realise now there must have been other voices, inside and outside Council, for example in the heads and on the lips of those doing planning and design, who realised that putting a crossing on the road wouldn't fix the problem. That what was needed was a bigger solution and a bigger budget.

And I also thought about that hall and the large fields that served that housing estate of maybe 500 people, and served in the weekend the cricketers (who were largely of a different culture and class), and I thought about how lucky we were. For a lot of the new intensive housing nowadays both in the centre and suburbs of the city seems to be premised on the assumption that either existing community facilities are adequate or that what we had in the past isn't needed as much. The new housing areas cram people in, provide little parking, little greenery, garden, or trees.

This is a community planning and design issue, and a mental health and wellbeing issue. But it's also a spiritual issue. How are spirits nurtured and revived? What space, what quiet, what water or bush, do we need? How do our living and community environments nurture good relationships, and help us care for the vulnerable among us? We need space to relate, to feel connected and whole, to think and to dream together.

A geographer friend told me about some research on how kids valued opportunistic '3rd places' in the city and this included trees (for sitting under, climbing, etc). The researchers gathered information about children's use and experiences of nine Auckland neighbourhoods, suburban and inner-city, using trip diaries, child-led walk-along interviews and discussion groups. The children were neighbourhood key informants and co-producers of the knowledge. They listed things like: 'friends close by,' 'places to play,' 'amenities nearby' (like fields, halls, etc), 'quiet and peaceful places,' and 'school.'

I wonder if we put the needs of children at the top of our priorities for the planning and design of neighbourhoods and cities, and then funded those first, what our communities would end up looking like. Maybe protests, like painting crossings, would no longer be needed.

# Helping

SOME THOUGHTS on how to help those in poverty:

Language is important. The language of our body and our tongue. To help someone our language needs to convey respect. Even, especially, if they are in a bad place and are mirroring the badness of that place.

Be wary of using the word 'poor'. Saying 'I need some help' doesn't mean the person is helpless or will always need some help. In many cultures, 'poor' is a label that carries shame, blame and stigma.

Try not to presume. Poverty comes in many shapes, sizes and suburbs. For some, it can come suddenly, with an abrupt change in financial circumstances. For some it can come with violence – physical and psychological. For some, it can come with ill health. For some, it can come with isolation. Some are born into poverty and find – when trying to leave it – barrier upon barrier.

Be kind. If someone asks to wash your windscreen, give them a supportive smile, even if your windscreen doesn't need it. And some supportive coins if you have any. Think of how you would like to be treated if you had to humble yourself to ask a stranger for help.

Listen as best you can. But know there are many of us who find it hard to listen and understand, because deprivation hasn't been our lived experience. Or we are just too busy doing our own good things to connect with those for whom life is not good.

There are people and agencies who know a lot more about poverty than we do – its causes and what helps. If someone asks for a loaf of bread or a fish, give them a loaf and a tin of fish. But give too to groups and agencies that help people to achieve food security.

And give too to groups and agencies that help people develop skills, like gardening and fishing, and help people afford the tools and products needed to garden and fish. And give too to those that help folk navigate all the barriers, bureaucracy and discrimination that so often arise when someone tries to break with the poverty of their past.

It's not just groups and agencies. There are doctors, nurses, and social workers who recognise poverty in their clinics and wards, and many teachers who recognise poverty in their classrooms, and others too. They try their best, but often feel it's not enough. Poverty seems to be always hovering about, ready to suck the promise out of any good.

There are many children in Aotearoa New Zealand who know poverty. And, though it really helps, they need more than food to thrive. And, though really it helps, they need more than warmth and safety too. They need someone they trust. And, most of all, they really need someone who will put them first, their needs first, and their own needs second.

We know too that all the kindness we can muster, all the food and help we can give, and all the financial and moral support to groups and agencies directly involved, won't make a lasting difference unless there is significant structural change in our society. For the uncomfortable truth is that the default settings on our society benefit those who already have, and not those who don't.

Changes in housing, employment, wage rates, food, and healthcare, including dismantling racism and sexism, need political solutions. And political solutions need the willingness of the majority to try something different, something which may cost them.

In the end, there's a choice to be made about the sort of society, country, we want to be. Do we want to be one where everyone is valued, everyone can participate, and everyone has enough? And, if so, are we prepared to make the far-reaching changes to make this possible?

# Pink Tulle

IT WAS SCHOOL HOLIDAYS. I saw them in the park. Mum and two kids jogging. The boy was a little older than his sister, maybe 11. And she maybe 9. Running as a team, mum in the rear.

They stood out. Not because they were jogging, or were a family group, or didn't have a dog. But because flowing out from the girl's hair-tie was a train of pink tulle that reached to at least her waist.

Bright pink. A statement. Hard to miss.

I could imagine the mother-daughter conversation earlier. A conversation where the mother insisted the children were going for a run with her. (The kids were too young to be left home alone.) The daughter responding with an 'only if I can wear my train'. And the brother rolling his eyes.

Of course, it might not have been like that at all, and the mother and brother could have been quite used to their jogging companion's different wardrobing ways.

As I looked at this little team, I smiled in thankfulness that there were girls in the world, and boys too, who want to embrace outlandish colours and wear what they will. They brighten up the world, and banish the boredom of the tyranny of fashion.

And I smiled in thankfulness that there were mothers in the world who embraced, and were secretly proud of, the eccentricities of their children. Mothers who defended the choices of their independently-minded offspring even if those choices would rarely, if ever, be their own.

And I smiled in thankfulness that there were brothers in the world who, when faced with pink tulle in the morning, weren't afraid to associate with their sister, despite what anyone else might think or say about them. Or sisters unafraid to associate with outrageously dressed brothers. That sort of loyalty is worth more than gold.

It is vogue these days to celebrate difference, to applaud and even plan for diversity. It's great to recognise the variety of cultures, genders, and families that make up the rich mosaic of many of our communities.

But often it is hard work. For with difference can come misunderstanding, with misunderstanding can come dissension, and with dissension can come harsh and hurtful words and actions. Such things can take years to repair.

Although children at times might lament being born into a family with lots of siblings and cousins, lots of personalities, and lots of differences, it is a gift. Managed well by parents and other adult relations, families are a great school for the cultivation of tolerance. For listening, before you presume and speak. For learning how to encourage, even when you disagree. For making each other strong and resilient, before any outside critic or bully tries to flatten you.

I stopped in the park and watched this little jogging family with the pink tulle flying. A minute or two later they rounded the bend and were gone. Maybe I'm wrong about my presumptions, but I'd like to think I'm not. The world needs more girls, or boys, to run with the courage of pink tulle, more mothers behind them, and more brothers, or sisters, beside them.

# Glimpses

**W**HAT DO WE KNOW, REALLY?
It is said to take a lifetime to know oneself, but now in my sixties I'm not sure I've arrived at many or even any conclusions. Rather, I catch fleeting glimpses, reflections in the mirror of friends or family, reflections in the puddles skirted or stood in. Glimpses when I've been at my best, my worst, and all between.

So, the statement 'I know myself' feels a bit too confident, certain and satisfied.

As does the statement that I know another person, no matter how close, over however many years. If we are lucky, our knowledge and experience of another is enough to build trust. And that trust is enough to build love. And that love is enough to bring joy.

We live with glimpses. Beautiful, precious glimpses. Moments to be cherished. Moments to be remembered, even when memory fails. Which, as we age, it does.

So, what do I know?

I know seeing the dawn makes my soul light. I too desire to break through the clouds and mist. And the sunrise tells me I can. Every morning can be Easter. Hope replenished.

I know when I get out of bed, my body kind of creaks. These days, it needs to get up and moving so it can keep moving. Old injuries and ailments need to be respected, respectfully worked around, and respectfully ignored.

I know that the dog is always pleased to see me in the morning. His wagging joy and slobber is like a grace that enfolds. And a grace before breakfast is needed for us both.

I know that I am loved even before I can think about it. The effect of that love is to brim me full of thankfulness. It is hard to overestimate the power of love, and its capacity to change everything.

I know that when I have suffered deeply there hasn't been a language to describe it. And that's okay. But it is immensely comforting to be in a companionable silence with someone who has also suffered similarly, or through a deep compassion knows what my soul needs.

I know that joy, and its manifestation, laughter, are two of the real treasures in life. As are those who make us smile, laugh, and feel good in it. Too often, though, we don't have long enough to savour such joy or such people.

Beauty gives joy. Aromas and tastes give joy. Music and dancing in the kitchen bring joy. A friend sharing stories brings joy. So too an inquisitive child. Feeling the wind blowing through what's left of my hair gives joy. As does the waving of the trees, and their endurance.

Today is an autumn day, a change time in the seasons. A time when we see endings and glimpse the possibility of beginnings. And in such times, it is steadying to remember what we know, what needs constant re-membering, and what doesn't matter if it's forgotten.

# A Puppy

LIFE IS A ROAD THAT SURPRISES. Again. Just when we thought we were on a long straight. Predictable, keeping between the lines, maintaining safe speed and following distance. The road not only turns but becomes a dirt track with bumps and things to avoid. Unpredictable. Adventuresome. Needing concentration.

And all it took was a puppy. By the name of Finn. His kennel name is one of Deep Purple's song titles, but we won't go there.

Now, I've had dogs (or been had by dogs) before. I know what it takes. Like early walks, and late ones. Getting to know the vet. Holes in the garden. Teeth marks. Mud. Poo. Affection. Play. I've had a dog to care for, off and on, for 28 years. I'm experienced. Seasoned. So, I should know what I've stepped in. Right?

And I've had one dog who hated on other dogs. You know, attacked fellow canines on sight. But was lovely with humans and cats and anyone else. Trust me, there is a small community of dog owners out there who walk at 5 a.m. Not because they like the dark and cold, but because they desperately don't want their dog to meet another dog. Only you probably don't know about such things unless it's happened to you. It's a very well-guarded secret.

Remember that classic dog movie *Marley and Me*? An out-of-control pup who grows with a family, dominates them, loves them, and is loved by them. You can watch it and think about all the things Owen Wilson's and Jennifer Aniston's characters are doing wrong. But you can also watch it and think: 'What if they tried to do everything right but it didn't work?' Which is a scary thought. A very scary thought. For the record, Marley didn't attack other dogs. Just furniture, walls, technological devices...

# A Puppy

Dogs, like children, do at times dominate our lives. They demand immediacy. 'What do you mean you're feeling tired? What do you mean it's cold, dark, and raining? Do you want 'you-know-what' on the kitchen floor? Get those shoes and coat on, you slacker, and let's get out of here!'

'Dominate' though is just one way of framing this. Another is that the dog is inviting us into a different way of living and being. Kind of like a new start, coming whether we're ready or not.

Like I have played more games of chasey and tug-o'-war in the last few weeks than I have in a decade.

Like when I go in to see him in the morning the first thing he wants is a cuddle. Indeed, he wants lots of cuddles all through the day. Fun fact: stroking a dog lowers its heart rate, and probably ours too.

Like I have walked around and sat outside our house more in these last weeks than I ever have. I have noticed the trees, the sticks, the leaves, and flowers more. I feel more 'earthed,' if that makes sense.

A friend of mine recently lost her soul companion. Her dog. It's hard to describe that kind of soul bond. You have to go on that journey yourself to know what it is.

And dogs, not surprisingly, are different from each other. It's not every dog in your life that will be a soul companion. But now and again, by the mercy of the fates or the alignment of the stars, it happens.

Then the road that began as a twisting, bumpy, dirt track becomes something else. More like you and the road become one, and the destination no longer is important.

As for Finn, he of Deep Purple origins, only time will tell.

# Mercy

"**M**ERCY!" A friend of my father's used to use the word as an expletive. A possible shorthand for 'may the gods have mercy on me who has to endure this nincompoop!', or something similar. As expletives go, it's preferable to most I hear.

There are certainly times we need a bit of mercy thrown our way. Like when installing a washing machine. Which I attempted to do last week.

First off, I had to remove the white beastie from our old house. I thought the attached hoses had to come too. Got one off, but not the second. Got son-in-law (eternal blessings on his being) and a big spanner on the job. He got it off. But I hadn't turned the water main off. Uh-oh! Yes, you guessed it, he got hosed and I was the nincompoop.

Secondly, I arrived at the new house. All loaded with spanners and washers and confidence. Screwed the hoses on real tight and... the outflow hose wouldn't fit. Drat! Confidence taking a plunge. So, I ring the plumber. He's coming tomorrow. The gods be praised.

Next morning, there's a big puddle on the laundry floor. Uh-oh! I turn off the water main and get mopping. Salvation is coming in the form of the plumber god, I say to myself.

The god descends. Those hoses from the old house didn't need to come too. The hosing of son-in-law needn't have happened. And my screwing them on real tight has screwed both the washers and the thread.

So, the plumber, radiating patience, gets me new hoses. Attaches everything just right. Even tests it. As he departs, he gives me an eyebrow of absolution, meaning 'it's fixed... now go and screw-up no more'.

The truth is we all need a good dollop of mercy in our lives. For all our nincompoop moments. Some of us more than most.

Joking aside, it is good from time to time to think about our screw-ups. Those times when we didn't listen well, think well, do well, or read the instruction manual. Those times when we supported a course of action that in hindsight was wrong. Those times when our ego knew best when it didn't. Those times when we thought we were on the right track but weren't.

It's good to think about these screw-ups not just to determine to do better but to admit to ourselves that we can do worse. That we have the capability to really make a mess of things, and sometimes do. And when we do, we might hopefully receive some mercy. Some kindness. Some help. Some forgiveness even. Like an eyebrow absolution.

And it's good to think about our screw-ups so that we might be less judgmental, less exasperated, and less scathing of others' screw-ups. Even when they're really bad.

Those old sayings like 'there but for the grace of God go I' and 'he/she who is without fault cast the first stone' are worth recalling. The former reminding us that the screw-up of others might have been ours. Their life of terrible circumstances and decisions might have been our life. And the latter saying, from a biblical story, reminding us not to condemn those who have been the recipient of bad circumstances or made bad decisions.

The world needs a lot of mercy right now. The mercy that is strong enough to withstand the ill-formed, misguided, malevolent, and violent thoughts and actions in many places around the world. The mercy that sees the good in the worst, and yet stands against the worst, calling it out, naming, shaming, and hopefully taming it. The mercy that knows deep down that we could have, given very different circumstances, been part of that worst. The mercy that holds tenaciously to a belief that goodness and kindness are more powerful than hatred and killing, even if the evidence seems otherwise.

# Trucks

6.30 A.M. Coffee in hand. The sky is at half-light. And Finn is looking out the window, contemplating.

I'm reading. Bits and pieces. Magazine and journal articles, online news, and the morning paper. I read a bit, sip a bit, and think a bit. It's a nice way to spend an hour before the day starts to get busy, and Finn tires of the contemplative life.

By the way, Finn's dad, Dexster, died last week. 320 messages of condolence were posted on his Facebook. If there's a heaven, dogs will be there running and chasing and fetching and loving. And Dexster will be in his element.

This morning, I'm reading the newspaper. I have a barely tolerable relationship with newspapers. They offer up the latest gloom – violent crime, heat waves, car crashes, price rises, politicians criticising other politicians, Americans shooting Americans... Newspapers aren't for the fainthearted.

I'm tempted to abstain from such news. And instead listen to podcasts, or read my favourite commentators, or just join Finn in his meditative practice.

On the other hand, I'm loathe to retreat into my silo and read or listen only to what I find agreeable. So, I read the paper, at least until it's fully light and time for our walk.

But this morning, there was a surprise waiting for me. A little gift from the newspaper gods to brighten my day and warm my heart. It was a story about a boy, Oliver, and trucks.

Oliver loves trucks. According to his mum, 7-year-old Oliver has always loved trucks. And, as with any ardent enthusiast, he knows his trucks. The little ones, the big ones, and the in-between. Their power, payload, and configuration. He knows every single name of every single truck and every single trucking firm. His mum says, "All he wants to do is be a truck driver".

His mum, wishing to surprise Oliver for his birthday, made a post on Facebook offering $50 to anyone willing to give Oliver a ride in their truck. But Oliver didn't get just one offer.

The owner of a local trucking firm saw the post and decided Oliver needed not just a truck, but a convoy of trucks. So he put a call out and 34 truckers responded. Word got around. So on the day, 64 trucks rolled up. Lots of the big rigs and then some. They came from miles around. Comments flowed in from around the world.

A trucking community turned out for this little boy. As the owner of that local firm said, "I would like every kid to know there is a community and people out there that will back them and stand beside them".

I suspect we all need, sometime in our lives, a 'convoy of trucks' to stand beside us.

It was a good day for trucks and all who drive them.

It was a good day for a kindness to be given to someone they didn't know.

It was a good day for children and all those grown-up children who love trucks and diggers and big mechanical toys.

It was a good day for the feeling of and making of community.

And it was a great day for Oliver.

# Readjustment

I WENT TO A FUNERAL last week. An old neighbour. I hadn't seen him in decades, and some of his children even longer.

The poet James K. Baxter, in his version of 'commandments', had one that said, 'Go to neighbours' funerals'. Baxter had a good list, and it's been far more relevant to my life than the ten attributed to Moses.

Not that you can command things like this. It's like commanding someone to love – you can't. Love must be freely given for it to be love.

I suspect wise ol' incorrigible Hemi* Baxter knew that going to funerals isn't just about honouring the dead and their family, meeting old mates, or revisiting your memories. It's also about having your memories readjusted.

Most of us only get a small peep at the life of another. We know them at school, or we work with them for a few years, or our children are friends with their children, or they are part of some group that we belong to. We get to know them, and sometimes think we know them well. But the truth is we know them only a bit.

Funerals often bring the bits together. Sometimes, the person we thought we knew has a whole other kind of life. The quiet introvert who barely said boo to a goose in the office was a poet and gave flowers regularly to his friends. The grumpy bugger we knew as a child worked for decades as a volunteer with the SPCA. The sweet little old lady we knew at bowls used to be a scuba diver and once had it out with a shark.

Yes, funerals are a great lesson in the maxim 'be slow to judge'. What we think we know ain't always so. What we think is so might be no longer though.

Funerals are also a great lesson in the fact that people are complex. Motivations are complex. And people do change. We might, for example, have seen a behaviour in someone's life that we didn't like. We don't and probably will never know why they did what they did. If that behaviour was hurtful we usually try to avoid them. But in another context, say with their children or grandchildren, they might be a loving and gentle person.

Which is why the old spiritual masters said, 'Do not judge.' Which is just another way of saying that most of us only have a small peep into the life of another, so let's be kind.

Let me say, in case you're wondering, my former neighbour who I knew when I was a child was not the harmful and hurtful type. Quite the opposite. He was a nice upright sober sort of guy, who walked to work every morning, was a bit stand-offish, and didn't yell at his kids (at least not in my hearing).

But at the funeral they read out a funny, leg-pulling piece that he had written to a grandchild. Well, I never...

And they read out a lovely, romantic, and deeply emotional piece he'd once written to his wife. Well, I never...

And they read a poem incorporating a spirituality respectful of Māori, our physical environment, and community. Well, I never...

Am I at the right funeral? Who was this guy??

My memory was having a readjustment. A good readjustment.

*Hemi is the Māori form of the name James or Jim.*

# Flowers

I CONFESS I DON'T KNOW much about flowers. I get confused about their names. I've never planted a flower. I don't know how to look after them. Sure, I know they need water. But how much and how often eludes me. I just hope they are hardy enough to keep growing and blooming, irrespective of my ignorance.

I also have no idea how to tell the difference between a flower and a weed. If it flowers, it's a flower, isn't it? Having read a little, I get the impression that flower versus weed is one of those debates decided by the personal preferences of those you associate with. Like what is 'good' music, or 'good' food.

What I do know about flowers is that I like them. They brighten the day. They say to sombre me, "Smile up". They say, "Congratulations". Or, "Happy Anniversary". Or, "Get better soon". For they make us feel good. They are unfailingly cheery. Like we'd like to be more often.

I wonder what it's like to work in a florist shop. To be in the business of trying to brighten people's lives. To arrange, collate, and give away beauty. A vocation of making people's worlds smile. Or maybe florists just think their job is buying and selling with a markup between. Or maybe, like so many in retail, the grind wears them down. And maybe their customers need to tell them about the difference they make to the quotient of happiness in the world.

In 2021, I moved house to the suburb of Onehunga. And, as is my wont, and Finn the dog's need, we walk the streets, usually first thing in the morning and last thing at night. Lots of streets. We meander, poke our noses here and there, pick up feijoas fallen on the footpath, give an acknowledging nod to other walkers, admire the big trees, and enjoy the variety of architecture and people who live in this eclectic neighbourhood.

And we notice the flowers. Some on bushes, like camellias. Some on vines, like clematis. Some adorning window boxes, like busy lizzies. And some houses, blessing upon them, plant their flowers close to the public footpath, cheering us up as we amble along. I'd like to think they do that deliberately. Cheer us up, I mean.

Some people also plant out on the berms, the public land between the footpath and road. Some plant shrubs, some flowers, and I've even seen a gnome or two. I admit I don't really get the gnome thing.

I enjoy how in this neighbourhood so many houses aren't secreted away behind high walls or hedges but have low fences or none, and offer their visual delights, their trees, gardens, and unique-cum-messy yards to passersby. They offer their botanical wonders, their emergent jungles, their wild gay bouquets, and in doing so they bolster the wellbeing of us all.

There is one lady, on my regular route, who is always out in her garden and, until recently, had this massive array of multi-coloured dahlias. By 'massive' I mean a stretch of garden the size of two cars! The month of May in the Southern hemisphere seems to be the end of the dahlia season, and she's out now planting bulbs and other magic.

Today, dog and I stopped. "Hello", I shouted. No response. "Hello", I called again. This time, she looked up and was hit by my best smile. "Hello", I said again, "I wanted to thank you for the beautiful flowers you keep growing so that people like me who walk on by can feel better and enjoy their day more fully". She gave a shy smile. And we chatted about what flowers she had planned for the upcoming months. I quickly got lost in the detail but kept smiling.

As I left feeling good, and seeing she felt good too, I wondered whether gardeners get thanked very often. Thanked by family and friends, or even by randoms and their dogs who pass by. Giving thanks, receiving thanks, and being grateful are all – like the flowers themselves – part of the magic that makes a place a good place, a neighbourhood a good neighbourhood, in which to dwell.

I hope urban planners, politicians, and those with the power and influence to structure communities think about these sorts of things and incorporate flowers and walking and talking and smiling and dogs into their designs.

# At One

THERE IS A PHRASE that sports people use called 'in the zone'. It refers to an athlete's mental state when they perform to the best of their ability. I've heard that some musicians use the phrase too. Artists as well. Sometimes our minds and bodies seem to align with the stars, and we feel good and perform physically or creatively very well.

That 'in the zone' moment can be a powerful five minutes, or a satisfying five hours.

Some years ago I walked the Milford Track. On the last day, my lot was to leave early, walk out, catch a bus, and get the car. So, I was up at dawn and heading out. The track was fairly flat. I got into a good breathing rhythm at a pace I could maintain, and the hours flew by. When I arrived at Sandfly Point (aptly named), I was feeling really good. I'd been in a great physical and mental zone for the last five hours. I hadn't tried to be super-fast, though I satisfyingly beat the track time by an hour. I had just tried to be constant, at one with my body and the environment I was in, at one with my breathing and state of mind.

Back when I turned 40, spurred by now-or-never thinking, I decided I needed to run a marathon. Set-a-target-and-go-for-it thinking. So, I got a program and trained religiously for six months. The time spent training was significant. Especially when we had three kids and another coming. I ended up doing two marathons and a couple of halves. My midlife crisis was satiated. The trouble was I didn't like running before I started all that effort, and I didn't change my mind along the way. I think now it was probably largely about vanity and self-flagellation.

Maybe I just never got fit enough to be 'in the zone'. To be at one with my body, my breathing, my moving, and the environment all around. Other runners certainly have in the zone moments.

Since that Milford day I've been thinking about other 'at one' moments. I remember once listening to a woman who studied one of the great masterpieces of art. For a PhD or something. I'm hazy on the details. I can't even remember which art piece it was. But I do remember her describing, after some months of study and gazing, a moment where she felt at one with the painting. I don't remember how long she said the moment was, but in a sense, it was a timeless. A clock-stopped, unforgettable moment of oneness.

Those who practise contemplation can also experience such things. It is as if the boundaries that usually define and limit us, namely our physical bodies and minds, are for a moment expanded so that our hearts beat in time with the heartbeat of the earth. It is difficult to talk about such things precisely.

Gazing at a beautiful tree, vista, or a wee flower, and finding oneself in the gazing getting lost in the beauty, is another way of talking about this at-oneness.

Giving ourselves over to a piece of music can do this too. Somehow, magically, we seem to be transported beyond our usual boundaries, and our spirits soar.

My guess is that many of us have had experiences like this and consciously or subconsciously we seek them out. For there is something very uplifting and re-energising about being in the zone, being simultaneously at one with our body and the body of the earth, with our mind and the larger presence and flow of creativity, beauty and wonder.

# Christmas

Dear Finn,

As an 8-month-old puppy, you are about to experience your first Christmas.

You will notice things that are different. Like that big tree in the lounge that doesn't smell like a tree. It is festooned with figurines, tinsel, and twinkling lights. At night, we turn the main lights off and the twinkles glow. It is called a Christmas tree, and it's not to be chewed.

The purpose of Christmas trees is that they have no purpose. They are just pretty. Beautiful. And beauty, like love, doesn't have to have a reason. Christmas trees appeal to that part of us that yearns to be transported away from our ordinary ways, away from work and worries, into an extraordinary imaginary fairyland. A place where dreams are good even if not true, but can come true when goodness catches on.

What's underneath the Christmas tree is the next thing to know. Hidden under the wrapping paper and ribbons are all sorts of nice things – like toys, books, food, and little things we never knew we needed or wanted. They are presents, gifts for others. A present is like a sign that says, 'I like you', or 'I care about you'. So, if the present is a box of chocolates say, the chocolates are really a message saying you're cared for and liked. Not that dogs should know anything about chocolates, mind you.

Most people – as they get older – like the other kind of presents, the one spelled with a 'ce' at the end. As we get older most of us prefer some companionship rather than more stuff to stuff our lives with. In dog language, and this might sound very strange to you, as you get older it's not what or how much you eat that's important but who you are eating with.

Such presence is the next thing you need to know about Christmas. You can't really do Christmas on your own. Christmas is a together thing. Together with family. Or together with friends. Or together with those who have no family or friends. It is a time for doing things for others. Mostly little things. Little kindnesses.

Christmas is about a belief in community. It says that no matter how poor or rich or needy you are, you belong. It says that no matter how bad or good or weird you are, you belong. It says no matter what you believe about God or Santa or politics, you belong. There's enough room for everyone. There's enough love and goodness to include everyone. But this depends on us. 'Peace on earth, goodwill to all' is up to us. Believing in Christmas is a commitment to making it happen.

Some of us like to go to church at Christmas. There we are together, and we sing and pray and ponder. We even go in the middle of the night when every good dog should be asleep. It's hard to explain why we go to church. In the old, old days, we had to. Now we just like to. We like being with each other. We like the feeling of this holy night.

Christmas is also a time for stories. The same story, told and re-told every year. A story about a baby, a mum, a dad, a journey, and visitors, stars, angels, and danger. A story where an unmarried mother is a hero, where gifts are given by strangers of a strange religion, and songs of unrealistic hope are sung. A story where class divisions seem to collapse, where owning a house doesn't matter, and finding room for a needy family does.

Christmas is a big story that tells us that goodness works, and works on us. Even when we can't see it. It tells us that bad things, like violence, greed, and loss, don't have the final word. Even when they seem to. And it tells us that when we're alone and wandering aimlessly, something strange – like a singing angel – can appear and turn our usual world upside-down. We believe these stories, even if the details are unbelievable. For these stories call us to be our best selves.

Singing is also a thing at Christmas. Some very beautiful music has been written especially for this time of year. This music is a language all of its own. It affects our mood in ways that words don't. It makes us receptive to wonder. It is a way the holy gets into the night.

There's even a Christmas song about a dog. Snoopy. Flying an aeroplane. You don't want to take too much of Christmas literally. For that song isn't really about a real dog in a real Sopwith Camel in a real dogfight. Instead, it's about the belief that there are things stronger and more powerful than war and hate. Things like friendship, honour and humour. Things that depend on us making them happen.

And lastly, there is food. Canine heart language. There are all sorts of Christmas foods to enjoy. Rich pudding, stollen, and mince pies. Chicken, salads, and kaimoana*. Turkey, ham, and lamb. You can really get stuffed at Christmas.

As you get older, you realise that the food is indeed a language. It is a language of hospitality that says that although the physical pleasure of eating is good, the physical pleasure of seeing others have pleasure is even better. And somehow the smorgasbord of it all – good company, good food, good feelings – served alongside the belief that doing and being good can triumph over all that rails against it – is very, very good indeed.

And this, Finn, is Christmas.

* *kaimoana* is a Māori word meaning seafood.

# Russ

RUSS DIED IN 2022. He was a minister. A character. Controversial. Different. Known to piss people off. Known too for going the extra mile. Sadly, I doubt that the likes of a Russ would get to be a minister these days. And we're poorer for it.

I can't remember when I first met him. I think he was in his garden, a big garden next to the church in Epsom. He spent a lot of time in that garden, attired in gumboots and hat, and people would come down the driveway and stop and chat to him.

He would light up his cigarette and lean back in the stance of a Yates seed agent talking to a typical Waikato farmer. He would nod, occasionally smile, encourage, and above all listen. Just as he'd done as a Yates seed agent back in the day.

He made a chicken coop in the vicarage grounds. The chooks were fenced in, but occasionally there were escapees. I heard that one of them made an appearance in church one Sunday morning to the consternation of some parishioners and to the delight of others, particularly the children.

Why he became a minister, I never asked. Why he was so loved, I'm not sure. But I guess it was because he kept close to people.

He also had political views at odds with most of his parish. It was the late 1970s and early '80s. He'd down his spade, put on his clergy collar, and march against nuclear arms, against racism, and against their underlying mythologies. He marched in 1981 against the Springbok tour. He got arrested at Waitangi in 1983. Some of the burghers of the parish wanted him punished. Younger members of the parish defended him.

He also signed up for the 'Clergy for Rowling' campaign. This campaign – difficult to understand these days – was more a revolt against the then incumbent Prime Minister's bullying and belittling style rather than necessarily an alignment with all the policies of Rowling's Labour party. Not that it was seen that way by many on the political right. It was a very divisive time in New Zealand politics, and Russ got off the non-aligned fence and got stuck in.

He got people thinking about the great issues of the day by taking sides, not by being impartial and leading study groups. You knew where he stood. And it wasn't where most of his parishioners stood. Though not many people left the parish.

He and his wife, Joan, believed in people eating together. And so, parishioners did. Those who liked him, those who didn't, all came to their table. So did youth group members who viewed his politics more favourably.

He was good at caring for people. Easy to relate to. He didn't have a big ego that bumped into you or tripped people up. Sermons were not something he gave a lot of time to, and the results showed. But his gardening anecdotes were memorable.

Russ also was one of those blokes who wasn't enamoured with committees. His Vestry meetings weren't particularly happy occasions. People would be elected to the Vestry with the intention of trying to keep him in line.

Russ was one of those people who, if he thought something needed doing, he just did it. Like the time he thought the hedge alongside the graveyard needed to go. He backed up the Holden, put a rope around the towbar and joined it to the base of the hedge, revved the engine, and let out the clutch. There was a lot of revved up discussion and reprimands at the next meeting of the Cemetery Board.

He also took a dislike to a couple of the leafy trees in the cemetery too and, like other men in the parish, enjoyed the gratifying roar and fumes of the chainsaw. There was more roaring and fuming discussion at the Cemetery Board meeting.

Mind you, the wood from those trees wasn't wasted. The vicarage had a massive fireplace in those days – a good 1.5 metres in length – and Russ had it going most of the winter.

In 1984, which must have been just a couple of years before his retirement, he took my ordination retreat. This sort of retreat, usually 5 days, is prior to being ordained a minister. Usually, too, there's lots of prayer, platitudes, and afterhours bonding with fellow ordinands. Though I can't remember too much of that stuff. I just remember the boat, and the fishing rods, and sitting out in Whangarei Harbour talking about nothing and everything and occasionally something.

In 1996, at the sesquicentennial of that Epsom parish, all the ministers back to the 1960s were alive and were invited. Each took a Sunday service and people came who'd known and appreciated them. Well, given all the grumbles I'd heard, I was pleasantly surprised to see how many people turned out for Russ – far more than for any other minister. Funny that.

# Weddings

ON A SUNNY WINTER'S AFTERNOON, the minister stands waiting at the front door of the stone church, bedecked in Presbyterian finery, smiling benignly and exuding calm, as the wedding guests arrive. It is something of an art to stand there, silent for the most part, declaring – in the mode of ministers – that all will be well, all manner of things will be well, even when they seem not.

This is no statement of misplaced faith. Quite the opposite. For, in the hour or so before standing with practiced calm, this minister has been busy. Doors unlocked. Lights on. Heaters on. Sound system on. Volume checked. Batteries checked. Furniture just so. Flowers checked. Organist duly greeted. Groom and entourage greeted. Anxious parents patiently listened to.

Not infrequently some parents have a last-minute wobble which manifests itself in things like wanting the childrens corner in the church to disappear, or the multi-coloured cushions to dematerialise, or the noticeboard disapparate. All those things that speak of the church being the home of a living community rather than a stone museum.

The minister knows these wobbles well and knows they have nothing whatsoever to do with children, cushions, or noticeboards and everything to do with a rite that publicly declares what the parents have long known (with a little fear), that their children are no longer their own. So, the minister meets such anxiety with knowing kindness, placating like a patient waiter, helping them get over the little things in order to do the big things well.

The biggest thing is being there, in every sense, for their child.

Sometimes, of course, the wobbles can lie elsewhere. With another family member. Or guest. Or groomsmen. Or groom. Or bride. Ministers like me who have presided at hundreds of weddings will always have a story or two to tell of wedding wobbles or worse.

I remember well one phone call the evening before. It's the bride. 'The wedding will go ahead', she begins resolutely, 'but there's been an accident'. I respond sympathetically. 'It's my fiancé; he's been run over'. Pause. Long pause. 'By my father.'

I gathered – over the course of the next day – that the father-in-law-to-be had been backing a trailer and somehow had collected his son-in-law-to-be. Who – topped up with painkillers – did manage to walk down the aisle with his bride, though I insisted that they both sit throughout most of the ceremony.

The blokes of course, in the manner of male solidarity, thought it was a great joke. The bride and her mother less so. The father-in-law wore a very penitent look all evening.

Then there was that time when waiting at the front door of the church I met a bride in physical distress. She didn't say anything. It was the look of her face. No colour. Skin kind of stretched. Bluish? Teeth clenched to stop them chattering. This was a very different looking bride than the one at the rehearsal the day before!

It happened to be a cold winter's day and she was dressed in a light white wedding gown. Not a cardigan or down jacket in sight. She and her beloved, following the advice of her photographer, had gone out for photos beforehand, posing in parks and on beaches. 'It was the light you understand.' But it was the cold the photographer didn't understand.

At the church door, the bride was bordering on hypothermia, and the usual tramping manual solution wasn't going to work. I promptly started the service, got her into church, and while the organist played on, wheeled two large gas heaters up close which began to thaw her out. As the service progressed, I could literally see her face change back into its usual shape and colour, much to my relief.

As I stood now on this sunny winter's afternoon at the front door of the church the groom was not drugged up and recovering from injuries and nor was the bride on the verge of hypothermia. Though I couldn't be certain about the bride, for she had not yet arrived. Yes, she was late. Only about 40 minutes late.

It is the lot of a minister to wait. There is no point looking agitated or grumpy, indeed it is counter-productive. So, you polish up the benign smile and attempt to exude that calm.

Not that the family were calm. They were buzzing around the front porch texting and tutting, and then ringing the driver and haranguing him in language I didn't understand and a tone I did.

One older gentleman, large in stature and voice, displaying rings on all his fingers and ears, was given the phone to make the authoritative call. I'm not sure who he addressed in the bridal car, but they were left with no doubt as to the error of their tardy ways and the punishment coming. I just hoped he wasn't talking to the bride.

As to the punishment, maybe mindful that he was standing within earshot of the minister, the time-challenged culprits were threatened that for every minute late they would be compelled to attend a church service!

I didn't quite know how to respond to that. So, I smiled, calmly continuing to convey the mantra that all will be well, all manner of things will be well, even when they seem not.

# Playing

I REMEMBER – some years ago now – visiting an elderly lady who liked to knit. That's what she'd do as we sipped tea and talked. She'd knit. Wool mittens, cardigans, and such like. Knitters are multi-taskers. Talking and knitting, sipping and knitting, seem to come naturally to such wielders of needles.

This lady, though, had a kitten. A kitten who liked to play with wool. It's in feline genes, I think. The kitten would start by dabbing at one of the balls of wool the lady had. The ball would move a bit. The kitten would dab some more. And the ball of wool would move some more. Before long, the ball had been moved quite a bit and the kitten was getting in a right old tangle.

At this point, the lady – and this is why it's stuck in my memory – instead of getting frustrated by the growing woolly mess, just smiled and gave a chuckle. And then, maybe seeing that I was smiling too, got out of her chair, knelt down on the floor, and picking up an end of wool dangled it teasingly for the kitten. The kitten, of course, always up for a new game, responded.

As I left her house, I was struck by the notion of pausing whatever we were doing, whatever serious business or conversation we were in the midst of, in order to bend down onto our knees to play with a kitten. Maybe if more adults – more busy, serious, important adults – took the time to bend down onto their knees to play we might be on our way to creating a happier, healthier world.

Certainly, the animals in our lives, if we let them, will always be up for play. Young children too seem to be wired for play. And play not just with contemporaries but with the adults in their life. The catch is that the adults often have to bend down onto their knees.

I was sitting in a doctor's waiting room the other day. The doctor I go to has two waiting rooms, both about equal size. One room has toys and children. The other has adults on their phones. So, I usually gravitate to where the toys are, in order to keep me off my phone, if you follow the logic.

A child was there with his grandmother, and she was on her phone. The grandmother ignored the child. Yet the child wanted the grandmother to play. So, time and again he approached her with a new toy he had discovered, and time and again he was told by a glare and hand wave to go away. They were both insistent – one to play and one to be left alone.

Now I can envisage all sorts of reasons why the grandmother did what she did, but to those of us looking on in that waiting room it was kind of sad. I thought about the joy of playing with children. I thought about the affirmation children get through playing with adults. I thought about how quickly children grow up and no longer want to play with any adults. I thought about what it would take for that grandmother to get out of the chair and onto her knees.

You may have heard of 'play therapy'. There are child versions and adult versions. The general idea is for the therapist to help the child, or adult, who might struggle with talking about their emotions or issues to express themselves through play. There's directive versions of play therapy and non-directive versions. And there's art, and Lego, and sand trays, and all sorts of good stuff. Maybe it's worth going to counselling just to give yourself permission to play.

Or you could get a kitten. Or a puppy. And in my experience kittens who when younger have been played with a lot never lose the desire for it. Similarly with puppies. They get wired for play their whole life long. I have the suspicion it might be the same with children. Although with children at some point some adult will come along and say 'put aside your childish ways' as if growing up is not meant to be fun, and play is only for the young, and seriousness is the mark of wisdom.

## Playing

For many brought up in the Roman Catholic and Anglican faiths to bend down onto your knees was a reference to prayer. It was taught as a posture of humility. (The origin of the word humility being 'humus', from the earth.) And in my upside-down religious thinking, when we bend down, when we move to be grounded, to play with animals or children, we are opening ourselves to a rhythm deep within. A rhythm of joy, a rhythm of longing to be expressed. Playing a prayer.

# Stocktake

As we get older, we begin to realise that at some stage there will be an end. The end, unwelcome though it may be, will come.

And so, some night when we're sitting idle, tired of watching screens and what passes for entertainment, we might begin to ponder upon some of those big questions: "Have I done what I've wanted to do in life?" "Have I been who I want to be in life?" "And if, by some miracle of imagination, I had my time again, would I do anything differently?" A kind of stocktake.

In my job, I go to a lot of funerals. Some of which I don't take. Funerals, as well as remembering the deceased and giving support to the family, are a good time to think about death. They're a good time to let your mind float free from the usual, imagine yourself in that casket, and do some pondering about what matters in life.

For the most part, if I had my time again, I wouldn't change a thing.

Which, for me, is quite a big statement. Because for large chunks of my early life I wanted to look different, have different parents, and be able to do the things that I thought only endless money could provide.

I wished I looked as cool as Joe, was as smart as Sam, and had parents that were the best bits of Robin's, Steve's, and Sally's combined. And my friends did too. They wanted to be cool, smart, and have reconfigured parents.

We were all just a tad – actually, probably more than a tad – insecure.

And we wanted things that cost money. Like cool clothes. Or money to go to any movie any time. Or a new bike. Or a car. Or to take a girlfriend or boyfriend to a restaurant. Or to have a holiday in Fiji, or Australia.

The endless money never came. But some clothes, movies, reconstituted bikes, bomb cars, restaurants, and holidays in tents did. Money was not central to our enjoyment of life, despite the messages that the marketeers of money continued to promulgate. Life was enjoyable all by itself.

Now I know that some people have really messed-up childhoods. Bad things happen. Things that their memories can't forget. Things that cripple their future. Things that left scars inside and out.

As far as I know, none of my classmates suffered from that kind of stuff. As far as I know. Which probably means in hindsight somebody did. But in the 60s and early 70s in my suburban sprawl street where we knew every neighbour, no back doors were locked, and no property was fenced, it felt like we were cocooned away from the nasty stuff.

That is not to say there weren't some bullies, and harassment, and fights, and hidings, and canings, all of which, most of which, got minimised or normalised. Which is a problem that now, decades later, society is trying to put right. Violence in whatever form should not be minimised or normalised or ignored.

If I did have my time again, I would like to worry a bit less.

I would like to worry less about what I looked like, compare myself less with others, and be more thankful that I'm me. And I would like to worry less about how I and others saw my parents, and be more thankful that they provided a home, food, and support. And I would like to worry less about what I didn't have, and be more thankful for what I did have.

For in those days what we did have was time. And fields, and beaches, and bush to walk, swim, and get lost in. And we had friends to walk, swim, and get lost with. We had lots of time to talk and try to piece together this great jigsaw puzzle called life. We had time to sit round camp fires, lie out under the stars, and watch the dawn break. We had time to dream small, big, or long. Without the distraction of anyone saying we couldn't.

What I didn't learn in those early days, though, was that friendships don't just naturally continue. You have to make an effort to connect and reconnect and do things together and be a part of each other's lives. So that's something else I would like to change if I had my time again.

Friendship is too valuable to be left to chance.

# NZ's Finest

THOMAS EVERTH is the owner of a picturesque sailing boat. A couple of years back, a picture of his boat featured in a large beer billboard attached to an office block in Remuera, Auckland. It had a large peace symbol on the mainsail. The boat, along with others, was part of a flotilla in 1995 that sailed to Moruroa Atoll in Polynesia to protest the testing of French nuclear bombs.

Lion Breweries, owners of the Steinlager brand, were using this incident, portrayed not only with billboards but a well-crafted video, to 'champion New Zealand's finest'. The inference being that both the protesters and the beer are New Zealand's finest.

When I first saw the advert, I was a bit surprised. Being on the fringes of the Nuclear Free and Independent Pacific Movement back in the day, I can't remember any large corporate organisations offering support or funding. And I would have remembered if Doug Myers, then CEO of Lion and well on his way to becoming one of New Zealand's richest, called a bunch of woolly lefty protesters New Zealand's finest.

The Steinlager version had a few kiwi blokes, and one woman, setting out on a daring adventure that brought French nuclear testing to an end. It is history condensed and sweetened. It doesn't include the ramming, boarding, tear-gassing, beatings, and blowing up incidents that the French Government sanctioned. Nor the tireless campaigning by Pasifika*, Māori, and Pākehā**, and the collaborations and alliances it engendered.

Throughout the long campaign – it started in the late '60s and ended in 1996 – to stop above and below ground nuclear testing, indigenous Tahitians were supported by a number of peace sailors and flotillas. The vaka*** Te Au O Tonga from the Cook Islands was there. Greenpeace was there. CND (Campaign for Nuclear Disarmament) was there. Even the NZ navy briefly joined in. It was not about a few Pākehā kiwis 'going their own way,' as the advertisement put it.

The Steinlager version also didn't mention the fall-out in the lives of the locals whose islands and bodies were radiated. There were 193 nuclear tests. The deaths number in the thousands. Many cases of radiation in Polynesia remained unreported for a long time. And the fall-out is not over. There is still radioactive mess. It is still messing with people's lives. It is still killing locals.

So, maybe not surprisingly, the NZ Advertising Standards Authority fielded complaints – complaints summed up in the catch-all phrase of 'it's not their story to tell'. Lion are probably wondering whether they should have stuck to their usual rugby players, suave caricatures of masculinity, and the like.

Which is why we might want to push pause on some of our criticisms. In the world of advertising vids you get a 90 second shot. You identify your market, you have a feel-good factor, and you create a story. You are not doing history, and certainly not accuracy. But you are presenting a snippet that the curious might want to follow further.

This perspective was summed up for me when I heard of a father being quizzed: 'Dad, what's that peace yacht thing about?' This was the first and only time I can recall that a big budget advert has been drawn on a peace, justice, and anti-colonisation canvas.

Thomas Everth didn't like his lovely two-masted boat being used in the campaign. He focused his criticism, though, on the product: alcohol. It isn't like Lion is selling insurance or breakfast cereal. Fiscally, the cost of alcohol harm in NZ is estimated to be $7.5 billion per annum. But Big Alcohol has New Zealand in its pocket, and most are content there. As a country, we don't appear to have the social or political will to curtail this drug.

So Everth, knowing this, suggested instead that Lion pay. $1 million. He wrote, "I am not letting (Lion) abuse the sacrifice and hard work of the hundreds of people who sailed thousands of miles to make our voices heard for selling a drug that is addictive and causes death, ill-health, and misery in our communities. I challenge you to make up for it, by donating".[1]

I applaud him. He's a peace and justice campaigner who is still campaigning. One of New Zealand's finest.

\* *Pasifika – used in New Zealand, referring to those who culturally identify with the Pacific Islands – principally Samoa, Fiji, Tonga, the Cook Islands and Niue.*
\*\* *Pākehā is a Māori word meaning New Zealand European.*
\*\*\* *vaka is from the language called Cook Island Māori – means canoe.*

---

1  https://thespinoff.co.nz/media/16-12-2020/this-steinlager-ad-distorts-the-truth-about-anti-nuclear-protest-in-the-pacific

# Blessed

IN THE LOCAL PRESS, there was a story about Anna, 37 years old, whose leg had been shattered into pieces by a hit and run driver. Recovery will be a long road. A hard and painful road, if full recovery is even possible.

The driver had been caught, arrested, and now was before the court. It will not go well for him. He'd run her down on a pedestrian crossing, then fled the scene.

I think of the near misses I or others I know have had. And those who weren't so lucky. Those who are living with bits of metal in their bodies, and aches, pills, or worse. It's a nightmare scenario.

Anna, though, is one of those exceptional people who has the capacity and grace to look past her own pain and injuries and extend forgiveness. She said to the reporter that she hopes the driver who hit her has support and kindness around him.

I know of the wisdom of forgiveness, that forgiving those who have hurt you aids your own healing and all that. I know the wisdom, but hey, this is really, really hard in practice.

And it's not like you just forgive once. Every time there is another operation, every time you can't do something you always used to do, every time the pain hits... there is the temptation to shout at him, to feel bitter, to wish he was suffering like you are suffering.

I don't really know how one learns or trains oneself to forgive like that. Being religious doesn't mean you're good at it, or worse at it.

I do know bitterness has to be let go of, rather than fed. But I don't blame anyone for feeling bitter. Especially not in a situation like Anna's.

I meet people from time to time who are travelling this hard rutted road of recovery that Anna's on. They've had to change their expectations of themselves and about what might be achieved in their lives. They live with limps, disfigurement, and lots of furtive looks.

But as stunning as Anna's generosity towards this driver is, it was what she said next that hit my heart: "I'm just so lucky, I feel really blessed".

Wow!

You could be forgiven for thinking she was loaded up on a mind-altering drug. Or was some sort of saint. "Lucky"? "Blessed"? Really?? Are you kidding?

One of the things I do is write blessings. I've yet to write one that begins with 'Blessed are those who have been run over and been smashed and broken'.

Yet that's what Anna in effect said. She was grateful that she was alive. And grateful that people loved her. She felt she was lucky. Blessed.

I've had the experience of being close to death and then waking up, alive again. Waking up was for me a really great feeling. And part of the reason was that I knew myself to be deeply loved. There was a feeling too that I got lucky. And a feeling too that I was blessed. I resonate with Anna.

But I hadn't been mashed up like her by some dingbat driver. I didn't really have anyone to begrudge or forgive. And I don't have the lasting effects that, sadly, I think she might be in for.

I suspect that calling yourself blessed though is, in the end, a decision. You can choose to delight in the glimpse of sunlight, or choose to yell at the prevailing gloom. You can choose to feel lucky, or feel cursed. You can choose to respond to the messiness of life with love and kindness, or with bitterness and remorse.

And for some, especially when the pain comes, it will be a daily choice, and a hard one.

# Quiet

I WAS TREATED TO DINNER out at a trendy restaurant on Ponsonby Road, Auckland. There was a queue at the door, exotic swells wafting out. Waiters bustled to and fro, squeezing between patrons. We were ushered to a pre-booked table where two stools awaited.

The aisle was half an arm's length. My back almost touched the back of the woman on the next table. It was the dining equivalent of being in a mosh pit.

The food was good. The waiter was great. The atmosphere was, in a word, loud. After about five minutes of effort, we gave up talking, looked at each other, and laughed.

All around us, people were having shouting conversations. I think there was some music somewhere too. We literally couldn't hear each other. Maybe we should learn NZ's third official language, sign.

It was a bustling place, for those who enjoy the bustle, the feeling of activity, the noise of the many amplified, and the smell and sounds and sensations of packed-tight.

After realising we'd ordered too much, our smiling waitress (I think she had pity on us) put our food in a doggy bag, and we headed outside. Never had Ponsonby Road seemed so quiet.

Even though I know I'm now considered old, I liked having the experience of being assailed by the many and the multifarious. And I liked too the experience of stepping out of it into the comparative stillness.

One of the things about the Covid-19 Lockdown was the quiet. As I sit here now in my study, I can hear the noise of trucks on the street, builders banging, cars, and the children in the Kindy next door. When one stops and listens, there is a lot of noise going on. Lockdown halted all that activity.

What I don't hear in my study are the birds. But I did during Lockdown. Not only had the noise quietened so I could hear them, but they came into suburbia more often. Or was that just an impression? Maybe the stillness allows other forms of life that have always been there to emerge and express themselves.

As I write this, as if on cue, a young child next door has found the joy of banging a drum. He is in a drumming mood and it is relentless. And so on-topic that again I feel like laughing.

I wonder whether the art of spirituality is really about balancing bustle and quiet, busyness and stillness, and enjoying and giving thanks for the juxtaposition between the two.

Quite often I wake in the middle of the night, get up, and find a comfy chair to sit in. The bustle and busyness have gone to sleep. And the quiet and stillness are waiting to permeate my soul.

I'm sure some people who get up in the middle of the night (yes, talking around there's a community of us) have profound thoughts, or compose great letters, or dream great music. I don't. I just sit. Have a snack. Be polite to the cats. And sit some more. I just want the quiet.

Sometimes, in the quiet of the night, I recall the faces and conversations of the people I've met during the day. And not just people from the day. But people from the past, including the dead, come and visit. Therapists might call it processing. Religious people might call it praying. Those who come to visit in the quiet hours are kind of like the birds in the Lockdown – they mostly come out when the noise is gone.

We live with noise. It is the sound of liveliness. It is the activity of being together. It is the hubbub of relationships. It is the making of music, food, and bustle. It is to be enjoyed. It is a good of our living.

But it is also good to step outside into that other world, the world of quiet.

# Ahh, Music

I WAS TALKING TO A MAN who lived for a time – a few months or maybe longer – in a cabin cut off from civilisation. It was in some hills, in a forest, where only birds, insects, and the inclement weather came to visit. There was no electricity, no internet, and no neighbours.

There, surrounded by the beauty, silence, and solitude, he lived his rustic hermit-like life. He planted a garden, dammed the stream to make a swimming hole, cut firewood, and kept a journal. An *On Walden Pond* type existence.

When he decided to return to city life, the first place he went to did not sell burgers. Or ice-cream. Or indeed food of any kind. It was also not somewhere where he could buy a computer, a coffee, a phone, a book, or anything we might consider a necessity. Instead, it was a concert hall, to listen to a musical performance. And he told me he cried. As the sounds penetrated through his ears to his heart, his eyes leaked tears.

What is it about music that goes to the deep heart's core? What is its magic? There's a great line from Dumbledore, the profound wizard of J.K Rowlings' creation. "Ah, music", he said, wiping his eyes. "A magic beyond all we do here!"

Music is a magic that can inflame the passions, move the feet to a beat, and bind a community. It's a magic that can calm our conflicts, centre our complexities, and turn our cacophonous thoughts into a single serene river that as it flows gives life. Music has a power beyond words, laws, creeds, and all those things that try to regulate and contain. It is a language of its own. A way of its own. A power of its own.

Back a few decades ago or more, I would travel to Massey University to attend block courses and stay with some friends of a friend. Paul and Sally had a house on the edge of Palmerston North that housed their three kids and cats, and which the icy wind tried to blow down. They were very hospitable.

Every night, around 10 pm, after the kids were in bed, Paul would sit at the piano and play Chopin, Schuman, Beethoven, Debussy, Bach, Gershwin. For hours. I would fall asleep with this beautiful music playing, then wake an hour or two later and Paul would still be playing. The music penetrated my dreams, my soul, and I imagine the others' too.

Thinking back, it was quite amazing. And I never asked him why he played for so long, and so often, and what it did for his soul. I just took it as a gift, and I expect his children took it as normal.

Paul died too young. I still can't really believe he's dead. Some people are so full of life that if they died then part of the universe must have too. Maybe he went to the music, became music.

Thoreau, he of *On Walden Pond* fame, once wrote, "A thrumming of piano-strings beyond the gardens and through the elms. At length the melody steals into my being. I know not when it began to occupy me. By some fortunate coincidence of thought or circumstance I am attuned to the universe, I am fitted to hear, my being moves in a sphere of melody, my fancy and imagination are excited to an inconceivable degree. This is no longer the dull earth on which I stood".[2]

I've spent some time at Walden Pond, walking the route from Concord as Thoreau did with his friend Emerson. The pond is a small lake, surrounded by bush, and now with a big carpark for the visitors. Thoreau's cabin is long gone, the site marked by a pile of stones, a pile added to by passing pilgrims. But on the edge of the carpark a replica has been built. The interior of the cabin is smaller than most children's bedrooms.

---

2 Henry David Thoreau (1960). "*H. D. Thoreau, a Writer's Journal*", Courier Corporation, p. 91.

## Ahh, Music

Thoreau found room though to have his flute with him in that cabin. But more importantly he was, as he said, already attuned to the music of the universe. He wrote, "Music is perpetual, and only the hearing is intermittent".

# Backyards

For those who live in rental accommodation one of the regular features is the three-monthly visitation by the owner or agent. Like other things in life that you can't avoid, it's best to put on a smile and try to make the event worthwhile. So, Saturday was spent in the garden – mowing, pruning, sweeping – between the rain showers.

And filling in holes. Three of them. I tell myself I'm lucky there are only three, and they're small. Made by you-know-who with the four legs and boundless energy, when he felt like being a little crazy. Nothing that a bit of soil and a bit of grass seed can't fix.

And don't we all feel a little crazy at times! Indeed, I sometimes envy Mr Finn. Like today, out in the park, we are ambling down this expansive grassy slope glistening with dew when Finn has an explosion of exuberance. He takes off, gains momentum, then flips himself on his back and slides down the hill. If dogs could shout 'Woohoo!' he would have. Instead, he got up and did it again.

I smiled. And I noticed others in the park smiling. It's hard not to smile in the presence of unleashed joy.

The universe – says the great eco-prophet Thomas Berry – can only be explained in terms of an exuberant expression of existence itself. So, Finn was explaining the universe this morning.

Beauty and joy are all around us. In the magnificence of the trees. In the colours of the fallen leaves. In the unexpected poking its nose around the corner.

The other day it was an avocado. I was walking along this path, off the gravelled park track, when there it was. An avocado. Blown from an avocado tree. In case you're wondering, this is not usual in Aotearoa New Zealand. I have never seen an avocado let alone an avocado tree in any park or track I've been on. Until then. So, a little green gift met me on the track, unbidden, unexpected, a wee blessing.

The park I'm referring to is Monte Cecilia, and it has a long history, both Māori and European. A European family way back in the 1800s planted trees. Now huge. Wonderfully huge. Sometimes I feel very grateful to such rich folk sparing us from virulent suburban sprawl.

They also planted an orchard. And, I guess, tucked away over the back, an avocado tree. Interestingly, the Council plan for the park specifically mentions that any fruit grown on the trees in the park is for anyone in the community. I really like that. Pity the park doesn't have feijoa trees.

There's a famous Canadian photographer, the late Courtney Milne, who has photographed sacred sites all around the world. Sacred Earth is his best-known book. But he's also done a book about his backyard. For the sacred, he says, is right here, right now, just outside the window, waiting to dazzle us with its wonder.

There is something about our backyards, the ones outside our windows, or five minutes down the road, or a drive away, that invite us to go, walk, sit, and imbibe the beauty and wonder of it all. The poet Mary Oliver defines prayer as paying attention. And maybe that's what being in our backyards is – a prayer.

# Solidarity

PAIN IS SOMETHING we hope we can take a pill for and it will go away. And that often happens.

Other pain needs other sort of intervention before it goes away. Like surgery. Or physiotherapy. Or rest.

Sometimes, pain requires us to take pills for a long period of time. The pills might just take the sharp edge off, and the rest must be lived with.

Some people live with pain constantly. Difficult pain. And, although it's hard, they try to live as normal a life as possible so their health isn't the sole subject of every conversation.

Some pain is visible, or diagnosable, and some isn't. Sometimes nobody knows why people are in pain.

Some pain is in the heart, as well as the mind, as well as the body. Where pills seldom reach. And the pills that do aren't very nice.

There is no best or worst when it comes to pain. Pain is very personal. Not something to compare with others.

One of the things ministers do a lot of, but probably not enough of, is sit with people who are in pain. And as the years have gone by, I realise that it is the sitting and listening that is more important than the doing or talking. Though we certainly need at times doers and talkers.

By sitting with, I am simply offering some solidarity. I'm silently saying that I think they are a wonderful human being, worthy of love and all care. And I take their suffering seriously. This is my silent prayer.

And there is one myth from my childhood that helps me with this. It might seem silly but I like what the Tooth Fairy offers.

Most children discard the Tooth Fairy somewhere around the age of eight. They write the fairy off as nonsense. Their second teeth have come. The cents gained from the story have been spent. It was good while it lasted. Now on to other things. It's like an old cell-phone with no charger. Redundant.

Yet the fairy, she or he or them, performs a simple function, for no apparent reason, inspired by no apparent motive, save to inadequately compensate children for the pain they have endured in shedding a tooth.

The fairy leaves money as an acknowledgment that children suffer pain and that such suffering is as unfair as it is inevitable. The Tooth Fairy is a symbol recognising that we have undergone hurt.

Contrary to the critics, I don't think the Tooth Fairy myth is about reducing everything to money. Rather, I think it's about solidarity. I think it's about parents (fairies in disguise) acknowledging with the help of a gender-neutral imaginary being that their child has been suffering. And then offering a little acknowledgment of that.

Which leads me back to beside the hospital bed, or the lounge, or the park bench. Wherever I am sitting with someone who is suffering. I'm inadequately offering some time and presence. But the sitting with isn't about me. It's about the connection, the listening, the solidarity with one who is in pain.

And both of us are hoping there will come an end to it.

# Rainbows

A WOMAN TOLD ME that she didn't like how queer communities used the word rainbow as a self-descriptor. She believed that religion, specifically Christianity, had a patent on the word. She referenced the Noah story, and said the rainbow was a symbol of hope.

I empathised with her about language that we think means one thing and then somebody goes and uses it to mean something else. Happens to me all the time. Just when I think the meaning is clear about one thing, someone adds a new meaning.

Like the word G-o-d. I thought it was a done deal that it meant love for one another. A mutual, transformative, life-giving love. Good, beautiful, healthy stuff that no one could object to.

But then along come other people who tell me I've got it completely wrong. God, they say, is a big superman in charge – lord, sovereign, father, judge of the earth, and all that and all that.

And I'm left thinking, given that I don't want a bar of all that and all that, maybe I shouldn't use the G-o-d word at all.

So, I empathise with this woman. She looks at me a little strangely when I tell her about my God thoughts. I suspect she thinks the big super god is the only way to think about God. But she hears me out.

I then try to say something about rainbows existing before language and religion did, and how the story of Noah and that ark doesn't show God in the best light. But by then she's getting up and politely putting some distance between us.

The Noah saga – when you think about it – has problems. Like there are about 8 million species of animals on earth. More back then. Then double that number for 'two of every kind' and you are left having to construct a very, very, very big boat!

Finding two of every kind is problematic too. Like, for example, there are 65,000 hermaphroditic species.

Then think about what some 16 million creatures are going to eat for 40 days and 40 nights. Especially the carnivores!

Then, given this flood was meant to cover the globe, there is the repopulate the earth thing. From one family. Limited gene pool. Lots of inbreeding. Not good.

Then there are all the dead bodies when the flood waters abate. Too many to bury. Think of the smell. And the infectious hazards of dead bodies.

About now you'll be thinking, 'Give us a break, Glynn, we all know this is just a story.' Which is true, it isn't history.

Yet it's a story with a moral. And to find it we need to read to the end where Noah has PTSD, is drowning himself in alcohol, and cursing his grandchildren. The moral being that all this death and destruction, including the trauma visited upon the survivors, is the result of a terrible god who thought he'd punish humankind by killing most of them.

Note: sometimes religions pass on tragic stories in their traditions to warn us about dangerous gods and bad ideas. Not all stories are setting an example for us to emulate.

As for the rainbow, I agree with the woman I was talking to. It's a symbol of hope. Hope that we will never justify mass murder. Hope that we will find a better god than this one. Hope that every species, every person, of whatever race, religion, or sexual identity, will find a welcome home on this planet.

In my last church, we created a billboard to celebrate and affirm the Rainbow Community Church which shared our building with us. It gave a different slant on the words 'two of every kind'.

# The Tide

CENSUS STATISTICS have consistently shown – even before the Covid-19 pandemic – a decline in church organisations. Indeed, churches had been on the decline for many decades. This is the reality that attendees and leaders like me have lived with all our lives. Churches don't fit the capitalist mantra that growth is good, and the corollary that no growth is death.

Of course, there are lots of little blips in the statistics. I've been in churches where the numbers coming have increased. Sometimes through things the leaders have done, but usually not. Immigration can affect numbers. Niche appeal can too. There are libraries of books and gurus telling leaders how to grow their churches. There are all sorts of things to try, which many of us have, and some have worked, for a while.

The macro-trend in Western Christianity is clear, and has been for at least half a century. The tide is going out, slowly. On everyone. Regardless of theology, music, kids' programs or community engagement. And, like the tide, no one is to blame.

So, all the games of 'mine is growing and yours isn't,' and all the games of 'do this, do that, and you'll grow', are simply that – games played while the tide keeps pulling.

And the other thing is this trend of numerical decline is prevalent in most voluntary organisations. Like Rotary or the Masons or sports clubs or womens and mens organisations. The landscape of how we come together has changed, as has the time we prioritise for such. And therefore, the desire for and purpose of community togetherness is questioned by many.

An interviewer from the NZ Geographic magazine questions me about this. "Given that other organisations offer social activities, educational events, connections for families with others", he asks, "what is the purpose of churches? Are they simply a mix of all that with a religious mantra thrown in?"

Yes, I answer, a church is a mini social service centre largely run by volunteers. Yes, a church is a social place for all ages that anyone can join. Yes, a church is a school, an education centre, mostly specialising in how we treat each other. Yes, a church is a place to sing (where else is there public singing these days?).

I would also add, the purpose of a church is to offer a place to ponder, to grow gratitude, and to wrestle with the meaning of life.

I think there is great value in coming to a place in which to silence my usual thoughts and demands and just listen. And ponder the imponderables and the possibilities. And not try to figure it all out. For somewhere inside us we know the equations of success and happiness aren't what their peddlers tell us.

And I think there is great value in doing this pondering with others around me doing the same. And to do this in a place where for decades others have done the same. Where pondering has seeped into and stained the walls not only of the church building but of hearts and a collective consciousness.

I can't remember all that I said to the interviewer, or what he wrote.

The tide metaphor naturally has its limitations. I don't think, for example, it will come back in and churches will fill up again. But neither do I think the 'sea' – that spiritual quest for meaning and connection – has gone away. I just hope that some of the best things about churches will still be around in the future and available to those who seek them.

# A Pyx

IN 1985, I was ordained an Anglican priest. On St Andrew's Day. A good Scottish omen.

I'm not one who, like with a birthday, remembers and celebrates such occasions. Indeed, if you asked me yesterday, I would have had to figure out the year, and I would have forgotten the day.

But today I have in front of me a gift given on that occasion, with the date engraved underneath. It just needed silver polish and good deal of rubbing to reveal it.

The gift is a pyx. The name comes from the Greek 'pyxis' meaning box or receptacle. I wonder if Anglicans still use them. Mine is about the size of a pocket watch. Not that anyone has those anymore either.

A pyx is for holding a piece of consecrated communion bread, with a drip of consecrated wine on top. There's an art to how you combine the two without making the bread soggy. I wonder if priests are still taught such things. Not that it really matters.

Receiving gifts when you are ordained is not uncommon. People receive Bibles, stoles, hei tiki*, cookbooks, flowers, and the like. Ordinations have a celebratory feel about them. Sometimes I think too much so. For there is something solemn about this commitment. Something that should make one pause. Even be a little afraid. Sort of like standing on the edge of a cliff.

A pyx is about commitment and solidarity. In it you carry something holy – a symbol of both hurt and hope. You carry it to the home, hospital, or cell of one who is in need. You listen, smile, care, and try to console. In time, as you let go of singularity and merge into plurality, you can become that symbol.

It's a great privilege to sit and listen. I've sat on crates. I've sat on leather lounge suites. I've sat on hospital chairs. I've sat on metallic benches. I've sat on garden swings. I've sat in rooms where I could see my breath. I've sat in prisons. I've sat on park seats. I've sat in cars. I've sat on street curbs. I've sat in some of the wealthiest and the poorest homes in our land. I've sat and tried to listen to the words and feelings, and to what might be behind them.

Not that I think I do much. I'm not a dispenser of advice, good cheer, medicinal therapy, or biblical truth. Or of God for that matter. I don't bring God in that little pyx. I'm just there. Listening to the silences.

Not very useful in a world where everything seems to have to be of use. Not very useful in a world measured by success. I'm a symbol of uselessness in a growth-orientated, purpose-driven world.

If there is any rationale to going and sitting and being with another, it is simply to convey that I believe in them. I believe in them no matter how sad, mad, bad, glad, wonderful, or different they are. I believe in them not for what they've achieved or will achieve, not for what they do or have done, not for their use and outcomes. I believe in them simply because they are part of the human family. No matter how fractured and disconnected they are.

That little pyx symbolises all that. A tiny, fractured piece of bread for a troubled, fractured world. A fractured me believing in a fractured you.

I don't carry my pyx any longer. Haven't for decades. It sits in my drawer. Maybe one day, after I retire, I'll give it away to somebody who knows what it is and symbolises, and what ordination demands.

\* *hei tiki is a Māori phrase meaning an image carved usually from jade that is worn around the neck.*

# Disruptive Space

I ENJOYED VISITING the Hundertwasser Art Centre in Whangarei. First mooted in 1993, it took nearly 30 years to become a reality. Which says a lot about the shifting sands of local politics, public opinion, and acceptance of an avant-garde artist.

Friedensreich Hundertwasser was one of those interesting, edgy people who can enrich our world but, like others on the edge, are often contentious. He was different. He thought differently. He thought disruptively.

Walking around the Art Centre (to find the front door which is at the back), I walked over uneven tiled ground with the allure of bright colours and curvature beckoning. Hundertwasser called straight lines 'godless and immoral' and 'something cowardly drawn with a rule, without thought or feeling'. Even the climb up the three storeys of stairs to the roof garden required walking on these curved tiled steps. Hundertwasser called an uneven floor 'melody to the feet'.

Although his paintings are attractive, especially the mix of textures and the celebration of vibrant colours, I found the experience of his art-cum-architecture more spiritually satisfying. By walking, touching, and being in this non-linear, richly-coloured, alternate environment, my normal ways of seeing, and therefore being, were disrupted. Such disruption asks that profound question: 'What if...?'

There are some religious buildings that try to do the same thing. To ask that 'what if' question by the very nature of their design and their use of space, shape, and colour. Such a building is trying to get us to re-examine our usual, comfortable ways of configuring the world and our thoughts within it.

Le Corbusier's chapel in Ronchamp, France, is one such building. Another is Gijs and Van Vaerenbergh's see-through church in Limburg, Belgium. And, of course, Antonio Gaudi's La Sagrada Familia in Barcelona.

It's something of a miracle that these disruptive spiritual spaces ever see completion. For most religious buildings reflect the need to seat a particular number of patrons, have people paying attention to the front, be made of durable yet affordable materials, have reasonable acoustics, and have some inspiring or uplifting features. Apart from the latter, such features are often common to other public buildings like town halls, courtrooms and classrooms.

They are designed for the comfort that comes with familiarity and compliance. The knowledgeable leaders are expected to be on an elevated platform up the front to impart their wisdom to the gathered.

They are not designed to be disruptive to our normative ways of thinking. Or inspire disruptive behaviours. They are not designed to ask the question 'What if...?' They are not designed to encourage dreamers who envision and then work towards the radically different.

As far as I know, Hundertwasser never designed a religious building from scratch and saw it built. But seeing his work in Aotearoa – in Whangarei and Kawakawa, and seeing his work overseas – in Austria, Germany, Japan, and elsewhere, one can imagine the features. A church with a roof garden. A church in tiles, and rich colours. A church with paint brushes and mess. A church with spaces for the unusual. A church with composting toilets. A church designed to ask questions of us - the in-breaking of the ecological, the correlation between a building and the soul, between peace and visual ugliness.

I wonder how many religious buildings – to say nothing of other public buildings – Hundertwasser would describe as visual pollution. Visual pollution, according to him, being more poisonous than any other kind of pollution, for it kills the soul.

# A Kransekake

A FRIEND OF MINE, who is skilled in such things, was baking a kransekake. It's a cake but not as we know it. It's Norwegian. Kransekake translates as wreath cake. The cake is made up of rings, each one slightly smaller than the one beneath it. There are 18 rings. So, when completed it looks like a conical tower.

Each ring is made from almond flour, castor sugar, and egg whites. After an overnight rest, the dough is rolled into ropes then fitted into specially made moulds. The moulds are necessary to get the right size for each ring. Once baked, the rings are stacked, kept in place by icing, and sprinkled with icing sugar.

As you can imagine, to make one of these takes hours and hours. It's a labour of love. For special occasions. And the occasion she was making it for was a wedding of a special couple.

My friend is one of those interesting people who dabbles with a number of creative endeavours, but cooking is her forte. It was quite a gift she was creating.

As I marvelled at this cake being built, I couldn't help thinking that by late Saturday night it would be no more. This time-rich, towering, beautiful, sweet sensation would be cut, plated, tasted, appreciated, and consumed. Probably totally consumed. (I sampled a small piece and it was delicious!)

Some of the best things in life are transitory. Here for a short time, then gone. Like a rose blooming. Only in this case there have been days spent making the blooming thing.

One of the insights that can come with age and a sprinkle of grace is the sense that the things we create are finite. What we build will come to an end.

Sure, there are ancient ruins of buildings that date back to around 9,500 BCE but they are ruins, remnants of a civilisation that is no more. With time, whatever we build, will perish.

And it's not only structures, of course, but art and relationships too. Everything is finite. Here today, gone tomorrow. Here this century, gone the next. This is the backdrop to our lives.

To counter this reality many people and some religions look for permanence. They might say their God never changes. But if you read a book like *The History of God*, you discover that our understandings of the divine have and will continue changing.

We might say love doesn't change. It endures all things; 'love never ends'. But, eventually, it does. Over the generations, memories fade and words are limited in their translation of love. In 100 years or more, our loves will probably be forgotten by our descendants, covered over by the sprinklings of time.

Some people, religious or not, create an afterlife world, often seeking permanence. Others try to create that after-death permanence through affluence or influence. But in the end, this too passes away.

While some might become despondent about this backdrop of finitude, I regularly find many who don't. They simply delight in and cherish each day, each person, and each experience. Maybe they savour the moment more deeply because they know it will not last, or ever be precisely replicated.

Baking a kransekake for others is a symbol of embracing the finitude of each moment. Baking a kransekake for others is something enjoyable, but transitory. Something that brings a smile, but is consumed. Something that is offered away, given not kept. Something that adds, for a moment or more, joy to others and beauty to the world.

# A Laugh

OUT THE BACK OF BEYOND. Following the dogs over the hills, through the bush, and the wet. It's in the owner's manual for busy dogs: "Take me on long walks with lots of room to roam". It's what I try to do on Mondays. Today it's blowing and raining something wicked, and Finn and his friends are having a ball.

Coming home, getting short on fuel, we pull into this service station that looks like a country store that looks like a rundown house. I've been here before and the coffee was surprisingly good. So, I park by the pump, and wander in to order. The door is wide open but the place is in darkness. Hesitantly I call out, 'Hello?'

The elderly proprietor who I guess hails originally from India calls back, 'Don't worry about us, we're just making love back here'.

And his wife, fellow proprietor, sheepishly moves her head forward into the doorway light and with a bit of a smile looks at me.

He then quickly explains the power outage, says they can still take cash, but can't make coffee. Which, travelling only with cards does me no good, so I retreat outside accompanied by the memory of their grins.

Getting back in the car, I pause for a moment and allow the delightful aroma of their humour to filter through my rain-soaked exterior and I let out a chuckle. And as I drive down the road, I realise they have given me much more than any fuel and caffeine could. They've made my good day even better.

It's not the full story but sometimes when life rains on us, and we get soaked and cold and miserable, it is easy to slip into moaning. Think of the couple at the store. With a power outage they were losing money. They didn't get any from me. Or from the guy who was pulling in when I left. They could be cursing the power company, or the storm, or the government. You can blame the government, any government, for most things if you try hard enough.

There is a whole moaning business in our society. It's about thinking of the bad things, of which there are plenty, and bemoaning them. And finding someone to blame, of which there are plenty of candidates, and blaming them. And it's about feeling sorry for our hardworking self, and others like us, then getting in a huddle and grizzling together. There are radio stations, opinion writers, news editors, and others devoted to this moaning business.

Not that there isn't a place for constructive criticism and the calling of public figures to account. But many of the storms that hit our country are not of our making. Although how we respond to them is. And anyway, whoever said life was going to be storm-free?

In the Roman Empire in the 1st and 2nd centuries CE, it was common place for like-minded groups of up to fifteen people to regularly dine together. So, fellow tradies, fellow religionists, fellow migrants would meet to eat. Common people. One writer calls these groups 'Supper Clubs'.

I think of them as survival clubs. Cause if we think today's times are tough, for those who weren't Roman citizens, times back then were very tough. Life was precarious, often brutal, and short. The storms of violence, discrimination, food insecurity, poor health, forced migration, excessive taxation, and the like were a regular feature of most commoners' lives.

There was one phrase in the 'Supper Clubs' book that leapt out at me. People would 'intentionally exaggerate' the benefits of eating together. When life was tough, instead of moaning and generating more misery, people would intentionally exaggerate the good of spending an evening with others – relaxing, sharing, singing, and dining. And I guess cracking jokes.

I love the resilience of that elderly couple who ran that store in the back country. That couple who met the bad luck of a storm

## A Laugh

with their gumboots of good cheer. They laughed. Probably at my initial surprised look! They smiled. And the smile stayed with me. And it's still with me. And you know what? Next time I'm out that way, I sure want to go back to their store.